HALO AND HOVERBOARD NOT REQUIRED

How To Develop a Fully Human Spirituality

Ronald W. Higdon

Energion Publications
Gonzalez, FL
2024

Copyright © 2023, Ronald W. Higdon

Unless otherwise indicated, Scripture quotations are taken from the Holy Bible, New Living Translation, copyright 1996, 2004, 2007, 2013 by Tyndale House Foundation. Used by permission of Tyndale House Publishers, Inc., Carol Stream, Illinois 760188. All rights reserved.

Scripture quotations marked BARNSTONE are taken from *The New Covenant* by Willis Barnstone, copyright 2002 by The Berkley Publishing Group, New York.

Scripture quotations marked MESSAGE are taken from THE MESSAGE. Copyright @ 1993, 1994, 1995, 1996, 2000, 2001, 20002. Used by permission of NavPress Publishing Group.

Scripture quotations marked NRSV are taken from the New Revised Standard Version, copyright 1989 by the Division of Christian Education & the National Council of the Churches of Christ.

Scripture quotations marked SCHONFIELD are taken from *The Original New Testament* by Hugh J. Schonfield, copyright 1998 by Element Books, Shaftesbury, Dorset.

Scripture quotations marked TNIV are taken from the Holy Bible, Today's New International Version, Copyright 2001, 2005 by International Bible Society. All rights reserved worldwide.

Cover Design: Henry Neufeld

ISBN: 978-1-63199-871-3
eISBN: 978-1-63199-872-0
Energion Publications
P. O. Box 841
Gonzalez, FL 32560

Energion.com
pub@energion.com

Dedication

With deep appreciation, this book is dedicated to Henry and Jody Neufeld who are the driving forces behind Energion Publications. Their guidance, patience, counsel, kindness, and supervision have made possible the publication of other titles, including this, my tenth book, with their press. Without their untiring efforts none of the books would have come to fruition. It is with deep and abiding gratitude that I give this long overdue dedication.

Table of Contents

Why I Almost Didn't Write This Book 1

1	Why Do We Think We Need a Halo and a Hoverboard to Be "Spiritual"?	5
2	Why Is the Number of Forgiveness 7 X 70?	15
3	Why Does Matthew Portray Jesus as the New Moses?	25
4	"Do You Know What I Have Done?"	35
5	What Did Jesus Pray About?	43
6	Is God in the Hedge Business?	53
7	The Danger of Unrealistic Expectations	65
8	In the Here and Now of Life's Specificity	77
9	Fully-Human Spirituality Always Involves "Spirit" With a Capital "S"	89
10	Living in a Weedy World	99
11	Fully-Human Spirituality Involves the Uniqueness that Belongs to Each of Us	107

Bibliography of Quoted Sources 111

Introduction:

Why I Almost Didn't Write This Book

When I floated the idea for this book past a few of my friends, the initial reaction appeared to be one of confusion. (The origin of the term "hoverboard" comes from *Back to the Future II* where Michael J. Fox rides a self-propelled levitating skateboard.) Most of the questions raised can be summarized into one: "How can you possibly tie the word 'human' with 'spirituality'? I am in a constant battle to keep (in Paul's words) the 'flesh' from overcoming the 'Spirit' in my life. Your title is not so much a paradox as it is a contradiction."

I found the classic statement of that "contradiction" years ago in Barbara Brown Taylor's *An Altar in the World: A Geography of Faith*:[1]

> There is no substitute for earthiness. From dust we came and to dust we shall return…God did not make "man" in the second chapter of Genesis. God made *adam* – an earthling – from the *Adamah* – the earth. God made a mud-baby, a dirt-person, a dirt-creature. Then God breathed into its nostrils, giving it divine CPR, and behold! A living being arose from the ground.

Even after making preliminary notes for several months, I was ready to abandon the project until someone gave me a copy of *A Burning in My Bones*, the 2021 biography of Eugene Peterson (author of the much-acclaimed biblical paraphrase, *The Message*).[2] It is now one of my "must read" recommendations. It brought me back to the eleven books by Eugene Peterson I had read and enjoyed

---

[1] Barbara Brown Taylor, *An Altar in the World* (New York: HarperOne, 2009), 149-150.
[2] Eugene H. Peterson, *A Burning in My Bones* (Colorado Springs: Waterbrook, 2021).

a decade or more ago. I was especially drawn to *Leap Over A Wall*. Its subtitle is: *Earthy Spirituality for Everyday Christians*.[3]

Leap Over a Wall is an insightful and creative exploration of the complex life of David. An endorsement on the back cover literally leaped off the page: "Eugene H. Peterson...plunges with David into the earthiness of our humanity and finds, through David, vital lessons for an earthy, everyday spirituality." On my rereading of the book, I can attest that the author lives up to a promise on the inside cover: "Peterson enters Scripture's rich, gritty depictions of David's failures and victories, personality and character, strengths and flaws."

Here is a mind-shaking paragraph from the book:

> The David story, like most other Bible stories, presents us not with a polished ideal to which we can aspire but with a rough-edged actuality in which we see humanity being formed – the God presence in the earth/human conditions...(David) has little wisdom to pass on to us on how to live successively. He was an unfortunate parent and an unfaithful husband. From a purely historical point of view he was a barbaric chieftain with a talent for poetry. But David's importance isn't in his morality or his military prowess but in his experience of and witness to God. Every event in his life was a confrontation with God.[4]

In the life of David, Peterson found an "earthy, everyday spirituality." I have tagged David as the prime example of a "fully human spirituality". In the rediscovery of his book, my motivation kicked in (I like to think of it as leadership of the Spirit), and I took fingers to the computer keyboard, ready to tackle the subject that had brought so many raised eyebrows from my friends. Question: If you can't raise a few eyebrows, what's the point in writing a book?

It is with great hesitation that I share the following information. It's highly personal in nature and the temptation to get on

---

3   Eugene H. Peterson, *Leap Over a Wall* (New York: HarperSanFrancisco, 1997).
4   Ibid, 5.

the defensive is almost overwhelming. The college I attended had a religious organization on campus that sponsored many workshops and projects throughout the year. Someone once told me that the reason I had not been asked to serve in any leadership position was that "they didn't think I was spiritual enough." I was too taken aback to ask for further details and simply kept that bit of information to myself. The question I did not verbalize was: What does it look like when one is "spiritual enough"? That question has now resurfaced with much larger dimensions.

I found a similar question many years ago in the classic movie *Around the World in 80 Days*. The question comes in one of the opening scenes in an Employment Office where a recently discharged valet is pouring out his soul about the unreasonable demands that had been made on him by Philius Fogg: "The man is mad! He is a tyrant. He is so exacting in his timing of everything that he carries around two watches. His daily bath water had to be 1 foot 3 ¼ inches, no more no less. His morning toast had to be 83 degrees Fahrenheit, no more no less." The director ponders for a moment and asks, "How does one take the temperature of toast?" It sounded much like the question that continued to rumble around in my memory bank: "How does one measure spirituality?"

Jesus tells a parable in which one of the characters has his measuring tape out the day he goes to the Temple to pray. His comparative evaluation sets the standard: "*God, I thank you that I am not like other people – robbers, evildoers, adulterers – or even like this tax collector. I fast twice a week and give a tenth of all I get*" (Luke 18:11-12). Most of the hearers would have marked him as a truly spiritual person. Two brief phrases bring some serious questions: The Pharisee stood by himself and the tax collector stood at a distance (vs. 11, vs. 13). The tax collector's brief prayer is given with head down and fist pounding his chest: "*God, have mercy on me, a sinner*" (vs. 13). The upsetting conclusion of the story is Jesus' announcement: "*I tell you that this man, rather than the other, went home justified before God. For all those who exalt themselves will be humbled, and those who humble themselves will be exalted*" (vs.14).

Is it possible that a tax collector could be more "spiritual" than a Pharisee? Before we can answer that question, we have to know what we mean by "being spiritual". Although the New Testament doesn't give directions for taking the temperature of toast, it does have a great deal to say about spirituality. It all seems to begin with our relationship to God and other people. It all seems to begin with an accurate assessment of our humanity. It all seems to involve much more than rule-keeping and proper observances. It's a lot to unpack but I want to attempt it because the assessment I received on my "spiritual life" in college haunts me to this day.

As I write this book, I do not imagine myself in a pulpit or standing behind a lectern. I imagine sitting in a study (a word I carefully choose) having a conversation with my readers. I invite you to join with me in this conversation which is about many of what I term the "basics". You will find in these pages what in seminary would be called the "prolegomenon" to my theology, the context within which I deal with the issues of life and faith. "Prolegomenon" is simply a fifty-dollar word for "preface" or "introduction". It's one of those words the Scribes and Pharisees would have used to impress the crowds. Jesus would probably have said, "Let me tell you about some things you need to keep in mind."

I trust this book will lead you into your own exploration of the things in your faith that matter, that undergird your way of life, and that enable you to have a fully human spirituality. Each chapter is divided into two parts: The Biblical Foundation, and Some Ramifications. Each chapter concludes with A Verse to Remember.

Chapter 1:

Why Do We Think We Need a Halo and a Hoverboard to Be "Spiritual"?

The Biblical Foundation

The Whole and Nothing But the Whole

The problem I have found with too much Bible study is that, as Professor Dale Moody liked to phrase it, it reflects "Kangaroo Exegesis." It is simply the method of jumping all around in the Scriptures, finding passages that fit our thesis, and putting them together to make a theological proposition. What this process fails to do is to honor the first principle of Biblical interpretation: "the totality of the biblical witness." Almost anything can be proved by selective reading out of context and, in this case, the context is the entire body of Holy Scripture.

This means that to gain a proper understanding of any passage of Scripture, we cannot ignore texts which appear to challenge or contradict what appears to be a clear interpretation. Frequently, if we keep in mind the panorama of the Bible, we will find ourselves writing: "On the other hand," "Under different circumstances," "A later passage appears to tell us," "This does not reveal the full nature of the God we have come to know in Jesus Christ," "The big picture causes us to see this text in an entirely new way."

We do not find the Bible to be a book of "systematic theology." Neither does it always present to us necessary gradations and priorities. The selecting and ordering of the biblical material and the construction of it into a total picture of God and his will and works, is one of the chief activities of theology (no small task!) Theological statements are often preceded by: "The Bible says…." What should be added is: "The Bible says…as I have understood it, arranged it, omitted parts of it, and interpreted it to the best of my present understanding,"

All Scripture is interpreted in the light of the highest and clearest revelation we have: Jesus Christ. He stands above all Scripture as the Living Word. We read the Scripture in light of what we know and understand of him. We are not so much people of the book as we are people of the person! (Does this sound like heresy?)

The two great bookends of the Bible give us the focus necessary for understanding what is to be found within its pages: *In the beginning God* (Genesis 1:1); In the end God (Revelation 21:3) *God himself will be with them and be their God* (TNIV). The subject of the Bible is God and his continuing revelation of himself and his purposes to humanity. A common heresy, as old as the second century Marcion, is the teaching that the God of the Old Testament is not the same God we find in the New Testament. Marcion rejected the principle of the totality of the biblical witness and did some real kangaroo hopping – he hopped right over the Hebrew Scriptures and the rich context it provides for understanding the Christian Scriptures. It is too easily forgotten that the only Bible the first Christians had was what we have too quickly come to call the Old Testament. It was from these Scriptures that the first believers found their evidence for believing that Jesus of Nazareth was the long-awaited Messiah. "Christianity in its inception was not a new religion; it was a Movement of Messianic Judaism."[5]

Jesus was a rabbi who regularly taught in the synagogues: Mark 1:21: *They went to Capernaum; and when the sabbath came, he entered the synagogue and taught. They were astonished at his teaching, for he taught them as one having authority, not as the scribes.* His message was the basic message of John the baptizer: the Kingdom of God, the Rule of God. The Scriptures he taught from were the Hebrew Scriptures. Both John and Jesus were heavily into the prophet Isaiah. Luke cites John's usage in 3:4-6 and Jesus' use of Isaiah at his hometown synagogue in Nazareth (Luke 4:16-19).

---

5   Hugh J. Schonfield, *The Original New Testament* (Shaftesbury, Dorset: Waterstone & Co., 1998), 20.

These were living words of living Scripture; the messengers were not attempting to start a new religion but were attempting to bring to fulfillment the message and words of the Hebrew prophets.

You'll never be able to toss aside the major portion of the Bible as obsolete if you keep in mind Jesus' words in Matthew 5:17 – *Do not think that I have come to abolish the law or the prophets; I have come not to abolish but to fulfill.* The Christian movement began as a movement within Judaism; its proclamation was that the Messiah had come and his name was Jesus of Nazareth. There is no way to understand the richness of the Christian Scriptures without understanding the richness of the Hebrew Scriptures. Sidebar: If we believe that all Scripture is inspired, why do we find such difficulty taking the Hebrew Scriptures seriously?

Did the Word Really Become Flesh?

The Christian Gospel is bracketed by two great God-initiated events: the Incarnation and the Resurrection. Everything in the New Testament is anchored, one way or another, in these inexplicable "happenings." I have often called them the two great miracle bookends of the Christian message.

In Matthew 1:20-24, Joseph's decision to divorce Mary (who was pledged to him), is reversed when an angel counsels him not to be afraid to take her home as his wife. In the middle of that dream, the writer explains what is happening: *All this took place to fulfill what the Lord had said through the prophet: "The virgin will conceive and give birth to a son, and they will call him Immanuel" (which means "God with us")*. Although not given a speaking role in the Christmas story, Joseph always responds quickly to the angelic instructions. "God with us" becomes the fulfillment of Isaiah's messianic prophecy.

John's Gospel frames the Incarnation the same way Genesis frames the creation: *In the beginning God…* Verses one and fourteen speak of this new creation: *In the beginning was the Word, and the Word was with God, and the Word was God… The Word became flesh and made his dwelling among us. We have seen his glory, the glory of the one and only Son, who came from the Father, full of grace and truth.* That Word became flesh and, upon arrival, was placed in a feeding trough. This is the meaning of the Greek word usually translated "manger." In his translation, Barnstone gives this footnote: "Manger is a feeding trough for animals. Though a beautiful and evocative word, 'manger' has come, incorrectly, to signify the stable rather than the feeding box, which conveys a more extraordinary incident."[6] Schonfield provides this translation: *She bore her firstborn son, wrapped him round, and laid him in a cattle-trough…* (SCHONFIELD).

This was a real birth, by a real mother, in a real place, in a real time. This is no god descending from heaven in a cloud and showing up with a glowing halo and floating just above ground so as not to contaminate his divine status. Perhaps my favorite translation is*: The Word became flesh and blood and moved into the neighborhood* (MESSAGE). Many are embarrassed that the Incarnation means that the Son of God was a real person in every way. However, biblically that means everything. Hebrews 4:14-16*: Since, then, we have a great high priest who has passed through the heavens, Jesus, the Son of God, let us hold fast to our confession. For we do not have a high priest who is unable to sympathize with our weaknesses, but we have one who in every respect has been tested as we are, yet without sin. Let us therefore approach the throne of grace with boldness, so that we may receive mercy and find grace to help in time of need* (NRSV).

Mark portrays the humanity of Jesus throughout: Jesus is moved to anger (3:5; 10:14); he sleeps (4:38); he marvels at unbelief (6:5) and sighs deeply in frustration (7:34; 8:12; 9:18); he also trembles (14:33) and feels God-forsaken. Mark, however, just as plainly understands Jesus to be the Son of God: at his baptism – 1:9-11; at his transfiguration - 9:7; at his crucifixion – 15:39. In his hometown of Nazareth, after Jesus' teaching session in the synagogue, the reaction is rejection: "*Where did he get all his wisdom and the power to perform such miracles? He's just the carpenter, the*

---

6 Willis Barnstone, *Restored New Testament* (New York: W. W. Norton, 2009), 334-335.

son of Mary and brother of James, Joseph, Judas, and Simon. And his sisters live right here among us." They were deeply offended and refused to believe in him* (Mark 6: 2-3). "Just the carpenter" was their assessment of Jesus as just another human being like the rest of them.

In Mark, Jesus refers to himself as "the son of man." We use "Son of Humanity" rather than "Son of Man". "Son of Humanity" more accurately reflects the Greek term anthropos and emphasizes that it is Jesus' humanity, not his maleness, that is theologically significant. One of the first heresies the church faced was not the denial of Jesus' divinity but the denial of his humanity. This was termed "Docetism"; it was the idea that Jesus only "seemed" to be human.

The Religious Establishment of his Day Saw Jesus as Much Too Human

Jesus responds to this charge in Luke 7:33-34: *"John the Baptist has come eating no bread and drinking no wine, and you say, 'He has a demon.' The Son of Man has come eating and drinking, and you say, 'Look, a glutton and a drunkard, a friend of tax collectors and sinners.'"*

In a Wednesday night Bible study in my first church after seminary, the text was the first part of John chapter two where, at a wedding, Jesus turns water into wine. We had barely begun before a hand went up and a woman exclaimed, "Now we all know this was not real wine; it was welch-aide." Before I could think of a good reply, another woman spoke up: "No. We are told that the people wondered why the best wine had been served last. They would not have said this about welch-aide. I believe Jesus turned water into real wine – but it has been an embarrassment to me all my life." She would have been even more embarrassed to realize that Jesus made between 120 and 150 gallons of wine. Her reaction was not at all like that of Jesus' followers: *and his disciples believed in him* (John 2:11, NRSV).

Some Ramifications

Is Spirituality in the Eye of the Beholder?

> There was nothing about the Master that any but the keenest eye would see as out of the ordinary. He could be frightened and depressed when circumstances warranted. He could laugh and cry and fly into a rage. He loved a goodly meal, was not averse to a drink or two and was even known to turn his head at the sight of a comely woman. When a traveler complained that the Master was not a "holy man," a disciple set him right: "It is one thing that a man be holy. It is quite another that he should seem holy to you."[7]

For those of us in the Christian community, an ever-present temptation is that we "look" spiritual. Jesus never appeared to make this a priority in his decisions of what to do. Eating with tax collectors and healing on the Sabbath did not look very spiritual to the orthodoxy keepers of his day. Making a Samaritan the hero of his most famous parable (Luke 10:30-37) certainly went beyond the boundaries of recognized models. If the first question is "How will this look?", then the most important question is ignored: "Is this something I ought to do?" It is easy to let the judgment of the crowd (or certain individuals) be our criterion for behavior and theological, social, or political positions.

Big Sidebar: I am not giving a pass to blatant anti-social, irresponsible, or destructive behavior. I am not advocating the "I don't care what anybody thinks" philosophy. It does matter how the important people in our lives view our behavior. The significant persons in my life have always provided appropriate signals that something needed to be examined. What I am advocating is more in keeping with the advice from Marcus Aurelius: "Give yourself a gift: the present moment. People out for posthumous fame forget that the Generations to Come will be the same annoying people

---

7 Anthony de Mello, *The Song of the Bird* (New York: Image Books, 1984), 142.

they know now. And just as mortal. What does it matter to you if they say x about you, or think y?"[8]

It did not look right for a rabbi to invite himself to the home of a tax collector for lunch (Zacchaeus, Luke 19:5). I cannot image the number of "worthy" people in Jericho who would have been delighted to welcome Jesus into their home. Jesus deliberately and publicly chose an outcast as his dining companion; he deliberately and publicly shaped his ministry by association with the "wrong" kind of people, with people on the margins.. This is the look he wanted his ministry and mission to have.

Does It Always Correlate With Our Expectations?

> The Broker's Men entered from the left, in accordance with the theatrical tradition that "good" always enters from the right.[9]

This British theatrical tradition noted in a novel was one of which I was not aware. I was fully aware of the manifestations of it in the ordinary run of life. So many of our "acceptables" and "expectations" come with the territory in which we have grown up. "Good" always entering from the stage right and "Bad" always entering from the stage left provides one of those quick either/or categories that keeps us from having to wrestle with the possibility of ambiguity. It reminds me of a phrase I often heard in my initial years of pastoral ministry: "I know good preaching when I hear it." That usually meant that I had entered from stage left.

When Philip informs Nathaniel, "*We have found the very person Moses and the prophets wrote about! His name is Jesus, the son of Joseph from Nazareth,*" Nathaniel's response is immediate: "*Nazareth! Can anything good come from there?*" (John 1:45-46). He knew stage left when he saw it; at least, he definitely knew stage right. Nazareth was a little nothing place off the beaten track. How could God

---

8 Marcus Aurelius, *Meditations* (New York: The Modern Library, 2003), 110.

9 Hamilton Crane, *Starring Miss Seton* (New York: Berkley Books, 1994), 11.

possibly choose such an "undistinguished place"[10] as the entry place for the Messiah?

Philip offers no argument to counter Nathaniel's question. His simple, *"Just come and see for yourself,"* is the challenge to take a look. He could have said, "This is not what any of us expected but this is the discovery we have made." If I know how, when, where, and with whom God works, then I won't have to spend any time looking for anything beyond my expectations. The late John Claypool said on more than one occasion: "God's other name is 'Surprise.'" I would suggest that God is the God of the unexpected.

When we know where grace is to be found, when we know how God works, when we know the kind of people through whom God works, when we know what to expect, life loses the dimensions of exploration and discovery. Our world becomes smaller; we become smaller. Paul's reminder is explicit: *Oh, what a wonderful God we have! How great are his riches and wisdom and knowledge! How impossible it is for us to understand his decisions and his methods! For who can know what the Lord is thinking? Who knows enough to be his counselor?* (Romans 11:33-34). We need to do a lot of looking in the realm of the unexpected.

Does God Use Real, Ordinary People?

> Like so many western characters Joe had come to know, and despite his demeanor and his constant scowl and rancher uniform of long-sleeved shirt, hat, jeans, and boots, Frank turned out to be a bundle of contradictions.[11]

I have never found a phrase that better describes the biblical "saints" than "a bundle of contradictions." The "heroes" so many of us idolized as children we now discover were highly-flawed, real, ordinary people – a bundle of contradictions. Abraham, out of fear for his own life, twice passed off his wife as his sister. Jacob, the "Israel" whose twelve sons were the foundation of the twelve tribes,

---

10 William Barclay, *The Gospel of John*, Vol 1 (Philadelphia: Westminster Press, 1956), 76.
11 C. J. Box, *Breaking Point* (New York: G. P. Putnam's Sons, 2013), 184.

Halo and Hoverboard not Required

tricked his brother out of the birthright and deceived his blind father in order to receive the blessing that was due to his brother, Esau. Joseph was a tattle-tale of the first order and initially is described as a person no one would want for a brother. Moses had to flee Egypt because he murdered an Egyptian. David's double sins of adultery and murder are no small matter in God's book of offenses.

It is impossible to find any biblical saints who wore a halo and floated a little above earthiness on a hoverboard. None of them cast off their humanity when they responded to God's call for his unique mission in their lives. Even Paul confesses his struggle with his humanity that kept asserting itself against all of his attempts to "conquer" it. Romans 7:14-25 is my reference for this struggle. Some commentators maintain that this is the confession of a "pre-conversion Saul" but the context seems to me to be the present-tense Paul. For most of us, this is a struggle we know far too much about.

Whatever made us believe we could attain a level of Christian maturity that provided exceptional conduct (sort of like Mary Poppins' "practically perfect in every way") and keep our feet out of the mire and mud of everyday existence? It seems to me that those who felt they had done this were some (not all) of the Pharisees Jesus encountered in his day. The classic illustration is the Pharisee, going to the Temple to pray, and beginning by thanking God that he was not like other people – meaning his halo was on straight and his hoverboard was at maximum height (Luke 18:10-14). Joining him in prayer that day was a tax collector who prayed in his full humanity, a very simple prayer: *"O God, be merciful to me, for I am a sinner."*

With Whom Do We Most Identify?

> …maybe we don't find a lot of answers to life's tougher questions, but if we find a few true friends, that's even better. They help you see who you truly are, which is not always the

loveliest version of yourself, but then comes the greatest miracle of all – they still love you.[12]

The halo and hoverboard folks make very challenging dinner companions. We always feel less while our guilt and shame are the hidden agendas in the conversation. We know we don't measure up and, our big question is, do they really measure up to the image they are presenting? We all know that real relationships are based, not on the sharing of perfection, but the sharing of our common humanity. That's the basis on which we identify with each other.

Anne Lamott, in the above quote, calls the love given by those who know us best, a miracle. Initially, that is God's miracle: his compassion, grace, mercy, and love for all of those who come to him just as they are. No special religious or spiritual qualifications are necessary. We relate to God in our humanity; we relate to one another in our humanity. And in that humanity, God uses us, not in spite of our humanity, but in and through that humanity. How could we possibly understand others if we had no idea what struggles they were going through? Looking down on others may be an enjoyable perspective, but it doesn't provide the proximity to reach out and touch. Neither does it provide the proximity for others to reach out and touch us.

A Verse to Remember

> *Psalm 103:14 – For he understands how weak we are; he knows that we are dust.*

---

12 Anne Lamott, *Stitches* (New York: Riverhead Books, 2013), 34.

Chapter Two:

Why Is the Number of Forgiveness 7 X 70?

The Biblical Foundation

When Counting Doesn't Count

When Peter asks Jesus how often he should forgive (Matthew 18:21-22), he also gives a guess of seven times. The rabbis taught that the requirement was three times; Peter doubles that and adds one for good measure. He expects Jesus' commendation. Instead, he hears, "You are to forgive seven times seventy. I don't want you to keep count. I want you to become a forgiving person."

Jesus' teaching on prayer in Matthew 6:5-15 contains what technically should be called "The Disciples Prayer" instead of "The Lord's Prayer." John 17 records what can more appropriately be titled "The Lord's Prayer." An important part of that prayer is: *Forgive us our trespasses (sins) as we forgive those who trespass against us.* A better (and I believe more accurate) translation is: *forgive us our sins just as we have forgiven those who have sinned against us* (6:12). This is consistent with the alarming, and seldom read, words of Jesus which follow the prayer: "*If you forgive those who sin against you, your heavenly Father will forgive you. But if you refuse to forgive others, your Father will not forgive your sins* (vs. 14-15).

My interpretation of this warning is that when we refuse to forgive others, we have closed the door through which God's forgiveness flows to us. Another way to come at the text is: an unforgiving spirit is simply the indication of an unrepentant spirit. An unforgiving person is an indication of a person who is not in a healthy relationship with God. This is illustrated in Jesus' parable of the king who forgives a servant's debt of *millions of dollars;* then the servant refuses to forgive someone who owes him a *few thousand dollars* and has him thrown into jail (Matthew 18:23-35). When the other servants report this to the king, he summons the man he had forgiven with the reprimand: "*You evil servant! I forgave you that tremendous debt because you pleaded with me. Shouldn't you have mercy on your fellow servant, just as I had mercy on you?*" The unforgiving servant is then thrown into prison until his debt is paid. Jesus gives the lesson of the parable in 18:35 – "*That's what my heavenly Father will do to you, if you refuse to forgive your brothers and sisters in your heart*"

Can We Recognize Sin When We See It?

Many years ago, Gert Behanna spoke at a Pastor's Conference. After she related her story about three failed marriages and a life of drug and alcohol addiction, this sixty-year-old got to the heart of her message. Here are some excerpts from a recording of her presentation:

> "Whenever I talk about my past, I beg you not to say, 'What a brave little woman to talk about her sins.' Instead, whatever are your sins, put them in the place of mine. Paul says all have sinned and are guilty and I presume this includes you (great laughter filled the auditorium). Now that I have graduated to the Christian sins, I find these more difficult than sins of the flesh. When anyone gets drunk and falls down, I assure you they know it and if not, someone will be kind enough to tell them. But these snide little Christian sins: 'Am I proud of not being proud.' I recently discovered that I'm a snob about snobs. I look down on people who look down on people. If one of your sins is to look down on us on drunks, that will be just fine for a sin. And, oh, – self-righteousness! That's a peach of a sin – that will do just fine for a sin."

Then she added this kicker line: "I can't remember anywhere where our Lord forgave the Pharisees." My take: because they wouldn't put down their halos or get off their hoverboards.

The goal is not halos and hoverboards. Jesus plainly stated that he was after much more than the Pharisee's display of good deeds: *"How terrible it will be for you teachers of religious law and you Pharisees. Hypocrites! You are so careful to clean the outside of the cup and the dish, but inside you are filthy – full of greed and self-indulgence! Blind Pharisees! First wash the inside of the cup, and then the outside will become clean, too"* (Matthew 23:25-26). Jesus' basic complaint against certain Pharisees and Scribes was that they were not the right kind of people - inside. When you check out what the Bible calls the fruit of the spirit, you find yourself into the inner dimension of who we really are: *The fruit of the spirit is love, joy, peace, patience, kindness, goodness, faithfulness, gentleness and self-control. Since we live by the Spirit, let us keep in step with the Spirit* (Galatians 5:22; TNIV).

According to Jesus, some things are weightier than others. *"Woe to you, scribes and Pharisees, hypocrites! For you tithe mint, dill, and cumin, and have neglected the weightier matters of the law: justice and mercy and faith. It is these you ought to have practiced without neglecting the others"* (Matthew 23:23; NRSV). The NIV reads: *"You have neglected the more important matters of the law – justice, mercy and faithfulness."* "The 'weightier' matters do not refer to the 'more difficult' or 'harder' but to the 'more central' the 'more decisive' or (as in NIV) 'more important' versus 'peripheral' or 'trifling' ones."[13]

Certainly, a change in conduct is an important part of the life of faith, but that change begins within and works its way out. As has often been said: "Salvation is grace, and ethics is gratitude." There is no doubt that the Pharisees were some of the most righteous people of their day, but too many majored on that which could easily be seen by others. In the Sermon on the Mount, Jesus stressed that almsgiving, prayer, and fasting should *"be done in secret"* (Matthew 6:4, 6, 18).

Jesus' declaration of his followers as the salt of the earth and the light of the world (Matthew 5:13-16) immediately follows the Beatitudes, all of which speak, first, to the interior life, to the motivations out of which actions flow. *God blesses those (note the present*

---

13   Frank E. Gaebelein, ed., *The Expositor's Bible Commentary*, Vol. 8 (Grand Rapids: Zondervan, 1984), 480.

tense) who realize their need for him, who mourn, who are gentle and lowly, who hungry and thirst for justice, who are merciful, whose hearts are pure, who work for peace, who are persecuted because they live for God (5:3-10). These qualities describe the character and integrity of those whom Jesus describes as Kingdom citizens.

Which is the most important commandment?

When one of the teachers of the law asks Jesus which is the greatest commandment, his answer combines Deuteronomy 6:4-5 and Leviticus 19:18:

"*The most important one is this*: '*Hear, O Israel: The Lord our God, the Lord is one. Love the Lord your God with all your heart and with all your soul and with all your mind and with all your strength.' The second is this: 'Love your neighbor as yourself.' There is no commandment greater than these*" (Mark 12:29-31).

I call this a "Relational Theology" because nothing supersedes our relationship to God, others, and ourselves. When the teacher who asked the question comments, "*To love (God) with all your heart, with all your understanding and with all your strength, and to love your neighbor as yourself is more important than all burnt offerings and sacrifices,*" Jesus announces, "*You are not far from the kingdom of God*" (Mark 12:33). The three relationships stand above everything else, or, as some like to say, summarize everything else. Any rules and regulations that either separate or damage our relationship to God, others, or ourselves are not a part of the kingdom Jesus proclaimed had arrived in his coming.

Although the elder brother of the prodigal is a model of the obedient and faithful son, he gets universally low marks when the story is discussed (Luke 15:11-32). He has been faithful and dutiful while his younger brother has *been in a distant land wasting all his money on wild living* (15:13). When famine and poverty push the younger brother to desperation, he finally *comes to his senses* (15:17) and decides to return home. He intends to confess to his father that he has sinned and is no longer worthy to be his son. "*Please take me on as a hired man*" (15:19) is the job for which he wants to apply.

In the resulting reunion, confession, reconciliation, and celebration, the elder brother remains working in the fields, unaware of the return of his father's younger son. (He never refers to him as his brother.) A servant informs him of the reason for the music, dancing, and feasting. The story ends with the father pleading for his halo and hoverboard son to join the celebration. In his resentment, he remains on the outside because, what he has earned, his brother has received as an undeserved gift.

In his tirade with his father, he complains: "*All these years I've been slaving for you and never disobeyed your orders. Yet you never gave me even a young goat so I could celebrate with my friends*" (15:29 TNIV). The focus of his entire conversation is on himself and his role as the better son whose hard work has been ignored. This is certainly not an illustration of "joyful service." The story ends with the father attempting to repair the relationship between his two sons and, of course, his older son's relationship with him. It's all about relationships gone wrong and the father (who represents God) attempting reconciliation. What is so much more important than the elder son's hard work is his lack of love for his brother. He had done all the right things; the tragedy is he is far from being the right kind of person. The problem rests with who he is, with who he has become.

This Means We Cannot Be Judgmental Persons.

Matthew 7:1 is perhaps Jesus' most ignored teaching: "*Stop judging others.*" He immediately asks: "*How can you think of saying, 'Let me help you get rid of that speck in your eye,' when you can't see past the log in your own eye?*" (7:4). My paraphrase: "When you insist on judging others, you don't know how ridiculous you look. You're like a person with a log protruding out of your eye searching for those who have a speck in theirs. What is truly amazing is how many specks you have discovered while remaining totally unaware of the log. You have no idea how many specks it would take to equal the "speck-tacular" log you're carrying around.

The real tragedy Jesus is citing is similar to one he pictures in his parable of the Pharisee and tax collector who go to the Temple to pray (Luke 18:10-14). The Pharisee is a master at recognizing sin in others but the self-awareness that is demanded when one encounters God in prayer is totally absent. When Isaiah goes to the Temple to pray, his encounter is immediately evident in the first words of his prayer: *"Woe is me! I am lost, for I am a man of unclean lips…*(6:5 NRSV). Isaiah in his prayer is focused on his own sins because they have become all too apparent.

A fully human spirituality is quick to confess that we have not been given, under any circumstances, the role of a judge. Paul's words in Romans 14:10-12 (reflecting on the conflict over what is acceptable to eat and what day it is acceptable to worship) remind us of where we stand: *So why do you condemn another Christian? Why do you look down on another Christian? Remember, each of us will stand personally before the judgment seat of God… Yes, each of us will have to give a personal account to God.*

Some Ramifications

A Practical Suggestion

> Marcus Aurelius: "Leave other people's mistakes where they lie."[14]

After finding repeated accolades for the meditations of Marcus Aurelius, the Stoic philosopher and Roman emperor from 161-180, I decided it was time to get the book. I have found it to be an amazing collection of wisdom for living a positive, pro-active life. If you check out my copy of the book, you will find many comments and stars by those items I have found worth noting and remembering. One does not have to abandon one's faith in order to find some enlightenment in other places. This is not heresy; it is simply the belief that we need to be open to truth wherever it is found.

---

14 Marcus Aurelius, *Meditations,* 122.

Aurelius writes as a fully human philosopher attempting to meet the challenges and opportunities that come to all of us, not just one who happens to be the Roman emperor. A parallel to the above quote is this reminder: "It's silly to try to escape other people's faults. They are inescapable. Just try to escape your own."[15] So many things that become a part of the judgmental mix in life don't really matter that much after all. If a mistake is not harmful to others in any way, it is best to leave it where it lies. Every fault we spot in others does not need to be announced and paraded before as many others as possible. Ignoring many of the human foibles we can so easily see in others can bring unbelievable harmony and peace to daily living. One thing is certain: the more we call attention to the mistakes of others, the more likely they are to call attention to ours, many of which we have probably not even recognized.

A final quote from Aurelius is a good summary statement: "To live a good life: We have the potential for it. If we can learn to be indifferent to what makes no difference."[16]

From God's Perspective

> David's sin, enormous as it was, was wildly outdone by God's grace. We have a finite number of ways to sin; God has an infinite number of ways to forgive.[17]

I have no doubt that Jesus formula of forgiving 7 x 70 was based on what he understood about the Father's forgiveness. Jesus wanted us to become forgiving persons because he knew his Father was a forgiving God. The consensus of Scripture is that our sins can always wildly be outdone by God's grace, if we but open the door through which that grace and forgiveness can enter our lives.

In Jesus' parable of the prodigal son, the rehearsal of what the son wants to tell his father and the actual delivery of that speech, both begin the same way: *"Father, I have sinned."* When David is

---

15 Ibid, 97.
16 Ibid, 152.
17 Eugene Peterson, *Leap Over a Wall*, 189-190.

confronted by Nathan (interestingly enough - through a story), his immediate response is: *"I have sinned against the Lord."* The problem with the group of super-righteous Pharisees who keep confronting Jesus is that they appear not to be able to recognize themselves as sinners. Jesus nowhere promises forgiveness to those who fail to acknowledge that they need it. To be unforgiven is to be unrepentant.

Biblically, we are all in the same boat: *For all have sinned; all fall short of God's glorious standard* (Romans 3:23). To be human does not negate that we have been created in the image of God. To confess our sins does not mean we will become less. I agree with Eugene Peterson:

> In the Christian life our primary task isn't to avoid sin, which is impossible anyway, but to recognize sin...If we stay with the story – the God story, the David story, the Jesus story – before long the condemnation gives way, whether slowly or suddenly, to the surprised realization of grace, mercy, and forgiveness. We think that if our sin is taken away, we'll become less. What happens is that we become more.[18]

I believe that the "more" we become is more compassionate and less judgmental, thus, reflecting more of the image of God in us: *But you, Lord, are a compassionate and gracious God, slow to anger, abounding in love and faithfulness* (Psalm 86:15). Surely if we are the recipients of God's grace, mercy, and forgiveness, we look at others in a different way because we are different persons than we were before we experienced the power of God's gifts. Our perspective has been transformed.

Thinking in a New Way

Some years ago I read Doug Marlette's novel *The Bridge*, a story about a southern family and forgiveness. The narrator is Pick

---

18 Ibid, 189.

Cantrell who has an ongoing conflict with his grandmother. He describes her as one who did not mellow with age.[19]

> "Over time she honed her natural gifts for pettiness and paranoia to an artform. She fought ceaselessly with neighbors even into her eighties. She burdened her family with endless demands, temper tantrums, and rages, and confounded legions of physicians with phantom illnesses and ailments."
>
> Over the course of the novel, Pick and his grandmother have a falling out and stop speaking to each other. One of the family, Buzz, comes to Pick and makes a request. The following conversation ensues:
>
> Buzz: "If you're asking me what might smooth things over and get back on track with the rest of the family I'd say just make a trip over and apologize."
>
> "Why doesn't she apologize?"
>
> "She can't. You know that. She's just one of those people lost in her righteousness. If anything is going to happen, you're going to have to instigate it. You're going to have to step up. Be the mature one."
>
> "I can't do it, Buzz." "Why not?" "Because." "Why?" "Because…if I do, she wins." "Pickard son," said Buzz, smiling as he reached across the table and placed his hand on my shoulder, "You know as well as I do this ain't no contest."

In the matter of forgiveness, the ball is always in our court. All of the teaching Jesus gives on the subject begins with our initiating forgiveness. With our initiating reconciliation. With our speaking the first word for bridgebuilding. It's not a contest; it's not about winners and losers. It's about being the one who, with full awareness of how much God has forgiven, is the first to reach out.

A Verse to Remember

> Psalm 65:3 – *Though our hearts are filled with sins, you forgive them all.*

---

19 Doug Marlette, *The Bridge* (New York: HarperCollins, 2001), 129-131.

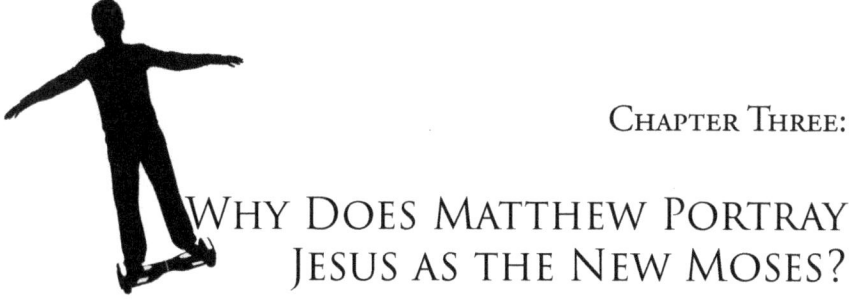

CHAPTER THREE:

WHY DOES MATTHEW PORTRAY JESUS AS THE NEW MOSES?

THE BIBLICAL FOUNDATION

Matthew is the Most Jewish Gospel

Matthew is the most Jewish of the Gospels because it was written for a Jewish audience. Its purpose is to present Jesus of Nazareth as the long-awaited Messiah, as the one the prophets had preached about and waited for. His readers (or most likely, hearers) are in mind when Matthew opens his Gospel with a genealogy that begins with Abraham.

Matthew sets what some consider his radical interpretation of Jesus ministry in the context of this clarification in Matthew 5:17 – *"Don't misunderstand why I have come. I did not come to abolish the law of Moses or the writings of the prophets. No, I came to fulfill them. I assure you, until heaven and earth disappear, even the smallest detail of God's law will remain until it is achieved."* And, according to Matthew, Jesus does this "fulfilling" as the new Moses.

Jesus is clearly pictured as the new Moses: Matthew 2:15 – *"I called my son out of Egypt."* The Law was given to Moses on Mount Sinai; Jesus delivers the heart of his message in the Sermon on the Mount. Matthew can be read in five sections like the Jewish Law (the 5 books of the Torah, the books attributed to Moses). Five times in Matthew the formula *"and when Jesus had finished these sayings"* marks a transition from one of Jesus' five major speeches to a narrative section recording his deeds (7:28-29; 11:1; 13:53; 19:1; and 26:1).

Moses, in some traditions, sits down to receive parts of his Law, as Jesus does to deliver his teachings in Matthew 5-7. It was common practice in the Synagogue for the rabbi to stand as he read the Scripture and to sit as he began his official teaching. Most rabbis, especially younger ones like Jesus, quoted authorities for their teaching; Jesus simply spoke with authority.

Jesus gives a new interpretation to the Torah. Three times (5:21,27, 33), he says, "*You have heard that the law of Moses says... but I say.*" Jesus reinterprets Moses, driving the external law of Moses toward the internal level of motivation. Rather than distributing a list of commandments, Jesus gave a single invitation, "*Follow me*" (Matthew 4:19, 8:22, 9:9; Mark 2:14; Luke 5:27). Moses had never proclaimed himself as the way, the truth, and the life as Jesus does in John 14:6. It should be remembered that the first designation placed on Christians was "followers of the Way". Truth as a person has a great many ramifications you will not find in truth inscribed on tablets of stone. The religion of the Pharisees who kept attacking Jesus, is seen in sharp contrast to 2 John 3: *May grace, mercy, and peace, which come from God our Father and from Jesus Christ his Son, be with us who LIVE IN TRUTH AND LOVE (emphasis mine).*

The New Testament is More Appropriately Titled the New Covenant

> New Covenant is an exact translation of the Greek *kaine diatheke* found in the Septuagint and in Paul's Corinthians 11:25 and Hebrews 8:8-13, meaning "new covenant." The title New Testament derives from *Novum Testamentum*, a mistranslation of *kaine diatheke*, appearing in the *Vulgata* (Vulgate), the fourth-century translation attributed to Jerome.[20]

The Bible speaks of relationship and community on every page. Its two parts are: Old Covenant and New Covenant. God takes the initiative to commit himself to people in the community known as Israel and then to people in the community known as church. (Jewish scholars maintain that the purpose of the Ten Commandments – "The Ten Words" or "The Ten Utterances" –

---

20 Willis Barnstone, *The New Covenant* (New York: Riverhead Books, 2002), 9.

is to create a redemptive community.) The covenants are built around two events: in the O.T. it is the slavery/exodus events; in the N.T. it is the cross/resurrection events. These are the two watersheds of Scripture. The signs of the Covenant are: in the Hebrew Bible – circumcision and community = Israel; in the Christian Scriptures – baptism and community = church.

In 2 Corinthians 3:6 we have the earliest record of the Greek words for "new covenant": (*God) is the one who has enabled us to represent his new covenant. This is a covenant, not of written laws, but of the Spirit.* Paul, no doubt, sees this as the fulfillment of Jeremiah 31:31 – *"The day will come," says the Lord, "when I will make a new covenant with the people of Israel and Judah… This is the new covenant I will make with the people of Israel on that day," says the Lord. "I will put my laws in their minds, and I will write them on their hearts"* (31:31, 33).

Although I disagree with much that Marcus Borg has written, Barnstone gives a quote of his with which I totally agree:

> Jesus was deeply Jewish. It is important to emphasize this obvious fact. Not only was he Jewish by birth and socialization, but he remained a Jew all of his life. His Scripture was the Jewish Bible. He did not intend to establish a new religion, but saw himself as having a mission within Judaism. He spoke as Jew to other Jews. His early followers were Jewish. All of the authors of the New Testament (with the possible exception of the author of Luke-Acts) were Jewish.[21]

Why Did Jesus Give the Eleventh Commandment?

The New Covenant was not the announcement that "anything goes." In Paul's writings, he found it necessary to provide a corrective word to those who felt that not being required to live by the letter of the law meant all requirements and restrictions had been lifted. Paul has a tough time explaining (and we have a tough time understanding) the relationship of Law to Gospel. Theologians never cease arguing over this subject. Some things are clear: *For you*

---
21 Ibid, 11.

have been called to live in freedom – not freedom to satisfy your sinful nature, but freedom to serve on another in love"* (Galatians 5:13).

In John 15:12 Jesus gives what many have called the eleventh commandment: *"My command is this: Love each other as I have loved you"* (TNIV). Jesus explains this kind of love in one sentence: *"I command you to love each other in the same way that I love you. And here is how to measure it – the greatest love is shown when people lay down their lives for their friends"* (15:9). Jesus had demonstrated that love when he assumed the role of a servant and washed the disciples' feet (more about this in chapter 4). He will shortly demonstrate the greatest love on a cross.

Ephesians 4:15 appears to be a frequently forgotten text – *Speaking the truth in love, we will in all things grow up into him who is the head, that is, Christ.* I once titled a sermon based on this Scripture, "Truth always walks a step behind love." This is in the context of our relationship with others, especially family and friends. Through Jesus' entire ministry with this group of disciples, love always had the priority. His grace, patience, and understanding, were always a part of his acceptance of them just as they were: misunderstanding much of what he taught, arguing about which of them was the greatest, anxious to have places of honor in the kingdom they were certain he was about to establish, ready to reign down fire at the first sign of rejection, careful to guard the superior position of their group (forbidding others to use Jesus' name in healing rituals), and rejecting the idea that it was necessary for him to die.

In Scripture, whenever any discussion arises about what is most import in life, love always comes up first. Nowhere is it better stated than in I Corinthians 13:13 – *There are three things that will endure – faith, hope, and love – and the greatest of these is love.* When Jesus is asked which is the greatest commandment, he does not hesitate to cite the two classics involving love for God, love for others, and, as I contend, love for self. This is another one of those ideas that sounds almost heretical until you remember that until we open ourselves to receive God's unconditional love for us, and experience that incredible acceptance just as we are, we will never be able to love God in return and to love others. If our bucket of love is empty, what do we have to share? Just check this out in your own daily experiences and ask when you felt most loving and accepting of others.

Feelings or Actions?

When Jesus asks us to love our enemies (Matthew 5:44), there is no way this could be a command to have warm, gracious feelings toward those who are doing us harm. Jesus spells out what it means in Luke 6:27-36 – "*Do good to those who hate you. Pray for those who hurt you…Do for others as you would like them to do for you…Love your enemies! Do good to them! Lend to them! And don't be concerned that they might not repay…You must be compassionate, just as your Father is compassionate*".

Jesus never commanded that we have warm, affectionate feeling for our enemies. Jesus is prescribing a set of actions that we can decide to take regardless of how we feel. A mark of maturity is evident when we are able to do what we really don't feel like doing but do it simply because it is the right thing to do. The end of the Sermon on the Mount is not a great "Amen!" but a tremendous crash. Where does this crash come from? Jesus concludes the sermon with this picture: "*Anyone who hears my teaching and ignores it is foolish, like a person who builds a house on sand. When the rains and floods come and the winds beat against that house, it will fall with a might crash*" (Matthew 7:26-27).

The Sermon on the Mount is basically teaching about the plan of action for Jesus' followers. It is a prescription for things to do regardless of how one feels. It is all about walking in the truth, walking in compassion, walking in the light, walking in the WAY. I have heard many voices raised for the posting of the Ten Commandments in public places. I have never heard any suggestion about displaying The Sermon on the Mount in any manner. The Ten Words Moses brought down from Sinai are basic to civility and culture but are not nearly as comprehensive as the actions called for in Jesus' words from the mountain. This being said, we need to keep constantly in mind Jesus words early in the Sermon on the Mount: *"Don't misunderstand why I have come. I did not come to abolish the law of Moses or the writings of the prophets. No, I came to fulfill them"* (Matthew 5:17).

Some Ramifications

Forgetting the Advent in Christmas

> A cartoon: A figure is leaning out of his car window at a drive-through. You see the golden arches in the background but the name across them reads "McChristmas." The man in the car is placing his order: "One 'Christmas Joy Combo' – supersized. Hold the Advent."[22]

Centuries ago, the church devised a cycle for the Christmas celebration. At the center was Advent, the 20-plus days beginning on the fourth Sunday before Christmas Day. It was a time of fasting, repentance, and abstaining from public festivities. The fasting and non-festive period would give way to overwhelming joy and celebration when Christmas Day finally came. Only then followed the 12 Days of Christmas, climaxing on January 6 with Epiphany, the commemoration of the visit of the Magi.

You'll never be able to get a Christmas Joy-Combo, supersized, unless you know what it is people of faith were waiting for. Unless you know just who has arrived. The meaning of the word Advent is "arrival." The writer of the Gospel of John knocks the socks off his readers when he announces who has arrived: one greater than Moses; one who has brought grace upon grace; one who has brought grace and truth; the only one who has ever seen God; *the one and only Son, who is himself God and is in closest relationship with the Father, has made him known* (John 1:18).

Almost everyone agrees that the first eighteen verses in John are nothing less that the revision of a hymn of the early church, a

---

22 *Christianity Today*, December 6, 1999.

hymn in four stanzas. In life and faith, some things are so grand and glorious, so magnificent and mysterious, that they can only be sung. Just the facts won't do. Some things are so wondrous that they burst the bonds of declarative sentences. That is why so much of the Bible is poetry and song. The message of the gospel is so big that it cannot be contained in mere speech; you have to sing it.

A New Approach

> He liked her, in spite of her reputation and the poor choices she had made. She had come to him the first time she was in trouble, and he'd tried to help her, but helping Monica back in those days was like trying to stop a freight train by standing on the tracks with his palm upraised.[23]

This description in a novel almost sounds like God's attempts to "get through" to his people since the very beginning. Covenants, laws, commandments, booming prophets, and sacrifices did not stop the freight train of disobedience and idol worship. There were many who told the truth of God's intentions for his creation. John tells us that grace and truth came through Jesus Christ. "Jesus didn't just say, 'I tell the truth.' Jesus said, '*I am the truth.*'"[24] "Truth is not a principle or a proposition but a Person. Truth is not rules and regulations but a relationship. God did not send us a statement but a Savior. God did not send us a principle but a Presence."[25]

Moses ascends to the top of the mountain and receives God's Ten Words (literal translation of Ten Commandments) – and there is thunder and lightning and smoke on the mountain. No one dares draw near except Moses. Jesus sits on the mountain side with the glory of God in him and all around him as the people gather on the mountain to hear him say, *"Blessed are the poor in spirit, for theirs is the kingdom of heaven; Blessed are the meek for they shall inherit the earth; Blessed are the pure in heart, for they shall see God"* (Matthew 5:3-8).

---

23 C. J. Box, *Blue Heaven* (New York: St. Martin's Press, 2007), 115.
24 Leonard Sweet, *Soulsunami* (Grand Rapids: Zondervan, 2001), 383.
25 Ibid, 385.

In the Old Testament and Jewish tradition, "yoke" was a common metaphor for servitude, and hence obedience. The rabbis often spoke of the "yoke of the Torah." In contrast to this tradition, Jesus says in Matthew 11:28-29: *Come to me, all of you who are weary and carry heavy burdens, and I will give you rest. Take my yoke upon you. Let me teach you. Let me teach you, because I am humble and gentle, and you will find rest for your souls. For my yoke fits perfectly, and the burden I give you is light."*

The term find rest literally means, "I will refresh you." I've lost the source of this, but it is most instructive: "Like 'rest' the 'easy' yoke of Jesus (the yoke that fits perfectly) is not an invitation to a life of ease, but of deliverance from the artificial burdens of human religion, which Matthew sees as a barrier to the true fellowship of the kingdom of God."

Where We Now Stand

The following is taken from the biography of Eugene Peterson, A Burning in My Bones:[26]

> One reason Eugene didn't wade into combustible issues was because in many instances, he'd not arrived at any definitive position on the matter. He was far more comfortable with ambiguity than most of us, and he generally assumed (a presumption many interpreted as naïve) that people of goodwill could honestly arrive at vastly different conclusions – and that we simply had to learn to live together in that awkward reality. Also, Eugene though that the hardened, absolutized positions of opposing theological poles typically framed conversations in ways that lacked wisdom, humility, and a Spirit-inspired way forward. He suspected there were better questions and wider angles than our intractable skirmishes…He wanted to leave the door open as wide as possible, open to as many as possible. He wanted to keep the conversation going.

Whether it is a matter of family, friends, religion, or politics the most important ingredient in maintaining a healthy relation-

---
26 Eugene Peterson, *A Burning in My Bones*, 282.

ship is to keep the conversation going. And that conversation is most important with those who have arrived at different conclusions on a variety of matters. It has always puzzled me why there is not a universal recognition of the fact that, throughout the history of the church, people have come to different interpretations from reading the same passages of Scripture; this ought to bring the realization that there are always better questions and wider angles. "The Bible says" has always meant: "My understanding of Scripture as I read this text is…" Early in the history of the tradition of which I was a part, one of the major tenets was "the right to fellowship across honest differences of opinion." Alas, that has changed both in the religious and the political world. Genuine conversation is at a premium. The right to a difference of opinion on issues has become a rarity. The dictum seems to be: "If you don't agree with me, you are simply shortsighted, ill-informed, and decidedly wrong." Aside from demonstrating a refusal to live with any ambiguity, it is the ultimate cut-off.

> The church (says Robert Farrar Capon) "has spent so much time inculcating in us the fear of making mistakes that she has made us like ill-taught piano students: we play our songs, but we never really hear them because our main concern is not to make music but to avoid some flub that will get us in dutch." (Then the book's author comments): "I have now heard the strains of grace, and I grieve for my friends who have not."[27]

I really believe the purpose of the gospel is to put music into our hearts, music into our souls, and songs on our lips.

A Verse to Remember

Psalm 58:11 – *Then at last everyone will say, "There truly is a reward for those who live for God; surely there is a God who judges justly here on earth."*

---

[27] Phillip Yancey, *What's So Amazing About Grace?* (Grand Rapids: Zondervan, 1997), 208.

Chapter Four:

"Do You Know What I Have Done?"

The Biblical Foundation

We're Still Trying to Figure It Out

The question Jesus asked his disciples in John 13:12, *"Do you know what I have done to you?* (NRSV), follows his washing of the disciples' feet, putting his robe on again, and returning to his place as their Teacher. It was a necessary question. We learn in Luke 22:24 that on their way to this "Last Supper," *they began to argue among themselves as to who would be the greatest in the coming Kingdom.* Earlier, James and John had made a request: In your glorious Kingdom we want to sit in places of honor next to you, one at your right and the other at your left" (Mark 10:37). When the other disciples learned of this request, they were furious (my translation). When Matthew relates this incident, it is their mother who makes the request (Matthew 20:20). Matthew may have wanted to paint the disciples with a brighter brush, but this still raises some issues. The problem remains: the disciples were all too human. Of course, this is the same "problem" that has always dogged the heels of all Christ's followers.

On the surface, what Jesus does is obvious: he assumes the role of a servant (or slave) and washes the feet of the disciples. I have theorized that the disciples, posturing for positions of honor in the coming Kingdom, were certainly in no mental state to perform such a lowly task. It would mean debasing themselves at the very time they were seeking just the opposite. It was a matter of dignity and prestige. They were not waiting to stoop to places of servanthood but were waiting to serve in new royal positions. Only Peter expresses the protest at the unspeakable act of their Master on his hands and knees before him.

Most translations miss an important note that should be re-inserted in Jesus' teaching. Jesus frequently uses something at the beginning of a discourse that we ordinarily think of being added at the end. We miss this in most versions because we get something like, "*Verily, verily I say to you,*" or "*Truly, truly I say to you.*" Three times in Jesus' explanation of what he has done (John 13:16, 20, 21) Jesus uses "*Amen, amen, I say to you*" as a prefatory to his remarks. "Amen, amen, I say to you, a servant is not above his master"; "Amen, amen, I say to you, anyone who welcomes my messenger is welcoming me, and anyone who welcomes me is welcoming the Father who sent me;" "Amen, amen I say to you, one of you will betray me". Jesus almost shouts: "Now hear this!"

The first "amen and amen" is our focus here as Jesus explains what he has done: "*You call me 'Teacher' and 'Lord,' and you are right because it is true. And since I, the Lord and Teacher have washed your feet, you ought to wash one another's feet. I have given you an example to follow. Do as I have done to you. How true it is that a servant is not greater than the master. Nor are messengers more important than the one who sends them. You know these things – now do them! This is the path of blessing*" (John 13:13-17).

Although some have taken this as the command to make this act an "ordinance" like baptism and communion, most see it in the context of the disciples' ambitions. Jesus insists that the path of blessing does not come by being served but by serving. It is not found in places of acclamation but in places of ministry. It is not found in places where others bow before us but in places where we kneel as servants. Jesus turns upside down all ideas of what it means to be great. *And the word became flesh and lived among us. And we gazed on his glory, the glory of the only son born of the father, who is filled with grace and truth* (John 1:14; BARNSTONE).

Whoever thought God's grace, glory, and truth would be symbolized by a towel and a basin of water? Whoever thought God's grace, glory, and truth would be symbolized by a cross? Paul puts it like this: *God…made his light shine in our hearts to give us the light of the knowledge of God's glory displayed in the face of Christ* (2 Corinthians 4:6; TNIV). *This is how God so loved the world* (John 3:16), this is how God revealed his nature and his purpose. This is what it means when Jesus is proclaimed KING OF KINGS AND LORD OF LORDS (Revelation 19:16).

It's An Upside-Down Kingdom

When Jesus talked about the "path of blessing" in John 13:17, he was, in essence, adding another Beatitude (Matthew 5:1-12). Most have difficulty believing that *"Whoever wants to be a leader among you must be your servant, and whoever wants to be first must be the slave of all"* (Mark 10:43-44). When Jesus discusses the wrap-up of history and time, he tells Peter: *"Many who are first will be last, and the last will be first"* (Matthew 19:30 NRSV). My preferred translation is: *"Many who seem to be important now will be the least important then, and those who are considered least here will be the greatest then"*. The ultimate standards of importance, significance, and success are not the world's standards.

Some discover too late that all they have sought and lived for proves to be disappointing and, frequently, empty. There are different versions of the children's story of someone (or some creature) climbing over everyone else to get to the top of the heap, only to discover that when they arrive there is nothing there. If it is all just "me, me, me" the result of my endeavors will be "no, no, no." *"Do not conform to the pattern of this world, but be transformed by the renewing of your mind. Then you will be able to test and approve what God's will is – his good, pleasing, and perfect will"* (Romans 12:1-2). Getting all I can, being number one, beating others at the game of life, seeking the seats of honor, being certain people look up to me, guarding my reputation, status, and position is a wearing and wearying pursuit. It often results in isolation, loneliness, and a loss of meaning and purpose.

Discovering the purpose of God for one's life begins with the discovery of whatever gifts we believe belong to us. The important questions are: "What do I love to do? What do I do best? What brings the most satisfaction in life? What gives me a reason to get out of bed each morning?" I remember reading the account of a man, in a nursing home, who was being interviewed about what had been the blessings in his life. He named his wife, children, and many friends and the many things in had enjoyed. But, then, he added, "What gave me the greatest blessing was that I was able to work at what I most enjoyed doing?" "And what was that? the reporter asked. "I was a paperhanger," he replied. Is it possible to hang wallpaper for the glory of God? Absolutely!

My favorite fully-human saint who reminds me of what it means to live in the here and now of life's specificity is Nicholas Herman. Nicholas Herman was a monk who lived more than three hundred years ago in France, He served as a soldier and then as a footman to the treasurer of the King of France. When he was thirty-eight years old something led him to the Carmelite monastery in Paris. The Carmelites took Herman in and he became a lay brother, working as a servant in the kitchen. He was never promoted. He always said he washed pots and pans for the glory of God. Better known as Brother Lawrence, the Kitchen Saint, he left a great number of notes and letters. His abbot, Joseph de Beaufort, published them after his death in a volume called The Practice of the Presence of God and it became a spiritual classic.

For too long in the history of the church, it was believed that "callings" were reserved for those in religious professions. "To be called" meant to enter ministry in some form. That left the majority of people simply "working" in "whatever." I have always maintained that everyone has a calling and to fulfill that calling is to fulfill one's purpose in life. Brother Lawrence was called to do kitchen duty. He became the Kitchen Saint the same way the man in our earlier story could be called the Wallpaper Saint. The "renewing of our minds" that Paul calls for in Romans 12, means that whoever and wherever we are, we can be Kingdom people. We can be people who love and serve in whatever role we feel is a fit for us. And we can bring dignity and grace and beauty to anything we are doing. There is nothing like getting out of bed each morning and repeating, "This is the day the Lord has made and I rejoice because I am able to do what he has called me to do." That is never a lowly task because there are no lesser tasks or lesser callings in God's Kingdom.

That day with a towel in his hand, Jesus glorified a job that was near the bottom of a servant's role. (I have often wondered if the next time the disciples gathered to celebrate the Lord's Supper, there might not have been a race to get to the towel,) Mother Teresa is worth quoting (again): "We are not called to do great things; we are called to do small things with great love." Picking up the sick and dying from the streets of Calcutta and giving them a bath and a place to spend their last days in care and comfort, could never be called a great work. But Mother Teresa turned it into a glorious work. The spirit, attitude, and the mind-set we bring to any task have transforming powers. Keeping that spirit, attitude, and mindset is not always easy but it is the path of blessing – not only for ourselves but for others.

SOME RAMIFICATIONS

How We See Ourselves and Others

Sir Cosmo Duff Gordon and Lady Duff Gordon left the Titanic with ten others in a boat that could have held forty. Newspapers carried this anonymous verse:[28]

> Did you
> Sir Cosmo Duff Gordon
> On the night of tragedy
> Behave as a gentleman or a coward?
> And restive hands
> Made so in regret of lost souls
> You might have saved

---

28 Andrew Wilson, *Shadow of the Titanic* (New York: Atria Paperback, 2011), 154-155.

But, for all craven and selfishness,
You did not.

The newspapers also carried Cosmo Duff Gordon's words in a court hearing:

> Question: "Would it not have been more appropriate, more in harmony with the traditions of seamanship, to suggest to the sailors that they try and rescue those who were dying?" "I have said that I did not consider the possibility – or, rather I should put it, the possibility of being able to help anybody never occurred to me at all." With these words, Sir Cosmo Duff Gordon had in effect damned himself.[29]

Such language only reminded the court of Duff Gordon's privileged position. The subtext of his testimony was that as Sir Cosmo was an aristocrat he need not worry about the welfare – or existence – of "lesser" human beings.[30]

The Titanic was divided according to class and most of those lost were third class passengers. One person in the classic Titanic movie was brazen enough to ask: "Will the lifeboats be separated according to class?" The implication of this comment is the basic assumption of Cosmo Duff Gordon: there were lesser human beings on the ship and they were not his concern. The big question, always under discussion: Is every person of equal value/worth in the sight of God? That question should have been answered in Jesus' life and ministry: he never found a "lesser" human being. There was room for everyone at the Kingdom table and there was no second or third-class seating.

In New Testament times, a servant (usually a slave) who washed the feet of the dinner guests never then joined the festivities. To repeat: I suspect that the reason none of the disciples had volunteered for this lowly task was because on their way to the Upper Room they had been arguing over which one of the was the greatest. There was no way they would shame themselves by grab-

---

29 Ibid, 161.
30 Ibid, 163.

bing a towel and basin. "I'm too good for that" was the unstated reason. A question that should have surfaced later that night: was Jesus a lesser Messiah and Teacher because he washed their feet? Did he become less because he became a servant? Is our value determined by our role in society, our financial standing, our level of education, our achievements in the business world, or the awards and recognition we have received? Our value appears to be a given and no one (or government) has the right to take that away from us.

Can We Do This?

> "We're just feeling our way, sir," said Blair, throwing a nasty look at Hamish, a look tinged with jealousy. Hamish's Highland lack of snobbery and his ability to ask questions of the rich and poor without making any difference between them always riled Blair.[31]

This excerpt from one of Beaton's delightful mystery novels, reveals why Hamish has so much trouble with Blair. Blair is quick to scrape and bow before the aristocrats and just as quick to ignore the "lesser" souls. He was, of course, jealous of Hamish and felt his own value in his profession overshadowed by one of his lesser staff members. I have always maintained that if we don't feel good about ourselves, we will never be able to feel good about most other people, unless we can place them in a lesser category of human being. What Jesus did in the Upper Room that night was to demonstrate his glory and majesty in his messiahship in a way that appears to be a contradiction in terms. Paul expresses it like this in Philippians 2:5-11:

> *Your attitude should be the same that Christ Jesus had. Though he was God, he did not demand and cling to his rights as God. He made himself nothing (laid aside his mighty power and glory), he took the humble position of a slave and appeared in human form. And in human form he obediently humbled himself*

---

31 M. C. Beaton, *Death of a Greedy Woman* (New York: Grand Central Publishing, 2011), 127.

even further by dying a criminal's death on the cross. Because of this, God raised him up to the heights of heaven and gave him a name that is above every name, so that at the name of Jesus every knee will bow, in heaven and on earth and under the earth, and every tongue will confess that Jesus Christ is Lord, to the glory of God the Father.

The reason Jesus could do this is that he knew who he was. His humility was not the "I am nothing" of so much false humility, but the actions of one who could fully and completely give himself to the Father's redemptive purpose. It is out of value, worth, significance, and purpose that Jesus finally dies a criminal's death on the cross. He was not a victim; he was the victor. His actions were all borne out of strength, not weakness.

A Verse to Remember

Psalm 43:3 – *Send out your light and your truth; let them guide me.*

Chapter Five:

What Did Jesus Pray About?

The Biblical Foundation

Jesus' Life and Ministry Were Saturated in Prayer

The next morning Jesus awoke long before daybreak and went alone into the wilderness to pray (Mark 1:35) After an enthusiastic reception in Capernaum marked by amazing teaching (1:22) and many healings (1:34).

Afterward he went up into the hills by himself to pray (Mark 6:46). (Following the feeding of the five thousand.)

Yet despite Jesus' instructions, the report of his power spread even faster, and vast crowds came to hear him preach and to be healed of their diseases. But Jesus often withdrew to the wilderness for prayer (Luke 5:15-16).

One day soon afterward Jesus went to a mountain to pray, and he prayed to God all night (Luke 6:12).

Many have suggested it would be helpful if we knew the content of these prayers. I believe what is more helpful is the fact that Jesus prayed often, alone, and frequently at great length. Jesus gave the example and taught that the most important characteristic of our praying should be its persistence. In Luke 18: 1-8, the parable of the widow and the unjust judge begins with this explanation: One day Jesus told his disciples a story to illustrate their need for constant prayer and to show them that they must never give up. In the story, the judge keeps ignoring the widow's pleas for justice but she keeps up her constant requests.

This is one of those occasions where Jesus explains the meaning of the parable: Then the Lord said, *"Learn a lesson from this evil judge. Even he rendered a just decision in the end, so don't you think*

God will surely give justice to his chosen people who plead with him day and night? Will he keep putting them off? I tell you, he will grant justice to them quickly!" The words "quickly" and "persistent" seem contradictory. However, it is a part of biblical wisdom to remember that time is relative when it comes to our calendars and God's purposes. Exodus 12:40 records that the people of Israel had lived in Egypt for 430 years. Although scholars debate this number, there is no doubt that the Israelites spent many years "pleading with him day and night "to deliver them from Egyptian slavery. Was their persistence effective? According to Jesus' parable, it was. Only our definition of "quickly" gets in the way of our agreement with Jesus' conclusion.

Most translations render Matthew 7:7 – "Ask, and it will be given you; search, and you will find; knock, and the door will be opened for you" (NRSV). The receiving, finding, and opening are promised fairly soon after the asking, searching, and knocking. In our personal prayer lives, most of us have found this to be something that takes time, sometimes, a great deal of time. I believe what Jesus intended to teach is much clearer in what I consider to be a better and more accurate translation: *"Keep on asking, and you will be given what you ask for. Keep on looking, and you will find. Keep on knocking, and the door will be opened. For everyone who asks, receives. Everyone who seeks, finds. And the door is opened to everyone who knocks".* It has been my experience that this is always true – with this caveat: What I receive is often not exactly what I was asking for – but I ultimately discover it is always better. What I find is not necessarily what I was searching for – but it is something I'm always grateful I have found. The door on which I was knocking is not always the door that opens – but what opens is always more liberating, expansive, and rewarding than I had ever dreamed of discovering. My confession is that from time to time, in the course of this kind of praying, I slip in another prayer from Psalm 13:1 – *O Lord, how long will you forget me? Forever? How long will you look the other way?* "How long?" reflects my timetable and my fully human spirituality.

The Model Prayer Surely Reflects Something of the Way Jesus Prayed

> *Once when Jesus had been out praying, one of his disciples came to him as he finished and said, "Lord, teach us to pray, just as John taught his disciples"* (Luke 11:1).

The preface (Matthew 6:5-8) to the prayer Jesus taught warns against parading prayer in public as the display of a halo and hoverboard religion. It is not meant to be a demonstration of how pious or devout we are. It is not meant to be a performance that puts us a notch or two above others. As demonstrated in Jesus' praying, it is not to be done standing in the synagogues and on the street corners to be seen by others but away from any audience. If we are honest, if we are really praying about what matters, most of us wouldn't want the things we need to talk to God about to be overheard by anyone.

In Jesus' model (Matthew 6:9-13), the prayer is addressed to our heavenly Father whose name we keep holy and sanctified. Prayer ushers us into another realm of reality where praise precedes all other matters we want to bring. What follows is not a rehearsing of our agenda but our commitment to God's Kingdom and God's purpose on earth. This is our priority; then we feel free to ask for the basics that sustain and nourish our lives. Recognizing our common humanity, we confess our need for God's forgiveness as we have forgiven those who have wronged us. This is a valid translation of verse 12 and parallels Jesus' shocking teaching in Matthew 6:14-15 – *For if you forgive others when they sin against you, your heavenly Father will also forgive you. But if you do not forgive others their sins, your Father will not forgive your sins.* Our forgiveness of others is the open door through which God's forgiveness flows to us. My free translation of verse 13 is: Give me the strength to resist temptation, and save me from situations where the evil is overwhelming.

In review: the "Our Father" is a prayer to be prayed and a model to be followed. Our prayers should begin with a recognition of the holiness of the God to whom we pray and the hallowed and sacred ground on which we stand when we say "Our Father." We always begin with praise and thanksgiving for the ways in which God has blessed and directed our lives. We commit ourselves to the fulfilling of God's will and purpose for us in our place and time in this world. Within this context, we feel free to ask God for the necessities of life or even those special things we feel we need to sustain a full and meaningful life. Then it is time to link ourselves to God's forgiveness and open our lives to the forgiveness we need even as we have already attempted to be those channels of forgiveness for those who need our forgiveness. We conclude with the recognition of how easy it is to miss the mark and fall short of the glory God intends for our lives. We ask for courage, his grace, and his Spirit in helping us avoid the dangerous pitfalls that would interrupt our faith-journey and create despair and discouragement instead of the joy and thanksgiving that should mark our lives as his children.

Sometimes Prayer Demands Profound Soul-Searching

> *And they came to an olive grove called Gethsemane and Jesus said, "Sit here while I go and pray." He took Peter, James, and John with him and he began to be filled with horror and deep distress He told them, "My soul is crushed with grief to the point of death. Stay here and watch with me."*
>
> *He went on a little farther and fell face down on the ground. He prayed that, if it were possible, the awful hour awaiting him might pass him by. "Abba, Father," he said, "everything is possible for you. Please take this cup of suffering from me. Yet I want your will, not mine"* (Mark 14:32-36).

Many are convinced this is Peter's eye-witness account of Jesus' prayer in Gethsemane where, shortly, *a battalion of Roman soldiers and Temple guards arrive to arrest Jesus* (John 18:3). John has no record of Jesus' prayer and Luke gives this version: *He walked about a stone's throw, and knelt down and prayed, "Father, if you are willing, please take this cup of suffering from me. Yet I want your will, not mine." Then an angel from heaven appeared and strengthened him.*

He prayed more fervently, and he was in such agony of spirit that his sweat fell to the ground like great drops of blood" (Luke 22:41-44). The NLT has this footnote for the two verses underlined above: "These verses are not included in many ancient manuscripts."

Only Mark and Matthew contain the agonizing details of Gethsemane; only Mark and Matthew record Jesus' cry from the cross, *"My God, my God, why have you forsaken me?"* There are 661 verses in Mark (the earliest Gospel) and Matthew uses 606 of these. Luke and John have "softer" versions of Gethsemane and words from the cross. Mark, as mentioned earlier, makes every effort to portray the Son of God in his full humanity. Our fully human spirituality is validated by these realistic and authentic examples of exactly how a real person would respond to the prospect and then the experience of crucifixion. "Contemporary writers describe it as a most painful form of death. The Gospels, however, give no detailed description of our Lord's physical sufferings, but simply and reverently say 'they crucified him.' It is this Christological aspect of the prayer that is given the greatest emphasis in the Gospels."[32]

There is no doubt that Jesus did a lot of soul-searching as he faced his final days. "Horror and deep distress" would be natural responses in light of the many crucifixions Jesus must have witnessed. His prayer also suggests that he wanted to make certain this was the way his Messianic mission was meant to be fulfilled. *For this is how God loved the world: he gave his only Son…(*John 3:16, NJB). This was the last and ultimate sacrifice to be offered for the sins of the world, and God provided it. Many theories have been offered as to exactly how the Atonement "works," but the Bible offers no definitive explanation. What is provided is the affirmation: *God was in Christ, reconciling the world to himself, no longer counting people's sins against them* (2 Corinthians 5:19).

Although many don't want to believe that Jesus would do it, for most of us in a similar situation, it would only be natural for us to cry out: *"My God, my God, why have you forsaken me?* (Mark

---

32 J. D. Douglas, ed., *The Illustrated Bible Dictionary,* Vol. 1 (Wheaton: Tyndale House Publishers, 1980), 344.

15:34). In noting that this is a direct quote from Psalm 22:1, many conjecture Jesus is asserting his faith and trust in God even in such a terrible moment. The Psalmist felt forsaken and there are times when almost all of us admit a time (or times) of feeling abandoned by God. Of course, God had not forsaken his Son but wouldn't it be natural, perfectly human, for Jesus to feel this way? And, of course, God has not forsaken us even in our most "awful hours" of loss and despair. To have such moments simply underscores the fully human spirituality that marks our lives.

SOME RAMIFICATIONS

Indications From the Jesus Prayer

> People try to get away from it all – to the country, to the beach, to the mountains. You always wish that you could do that too. Which is idiotic: you can get away from it anytime you like. By going within. Nowhere you can go is more peaceful – more free of interruptions – than your own soul...Renew yourself. But keep it brief and basic.[33]

We have already mentioned that The Lord's Prayer is more accurately called The Disciples' Prayer. What can truly be called The Lord's Prayer is the prayer of Jesus found in John 17. The content reveals the things that concern him as his journey in this world nears its completion. In his prayer, Jesus goes deeply within as he explores his commitment to his mission and especially his calling of disciples as a part of his master plan. In fact, most of the prayer is for them, that they will be faithful and enable others to know that he has been sent from the Father. His prayer that his disciples will be one has often been cited as the prayer that has yet to be answered. He reaffirms the love that the Father gave to him even before the world began. His concluding prayer is that the disciples may experience that same kind of love in their lives. It is no small matter than this prayer ends on the high note of God's love.

---

33 Marcus Aurelius, *Meditations*, 37.

In our own praying, as we go within, it is only natural that we voice our concerns about where we have journeyed in our lives, what we hope we have accomplished, and our hopes for the future. For most of us, this is also the time to reaffirm our belief in God's unconditional love for us. In workshops, I have often asked the participants to repeat John 3:16 and put their own name in the place of 'the world": *For God so loved (your name) that he gave his only Son...* My contention is that God's love is not a general "God loves everyone" but that God loves us individually by name. My favorite verse has always been John 11:5 – *Jesus loved Martha, Mary, and Lazarus...* That's what it means for God to love the world.

The Way to Avoid the Hyper-Present

> Today, in our tech-driven, device-addled, tweeting, texting, snapchating, linking, beeping, 24/7 newsfeed world, it is easy to get caught up in the hyper-present. It is easier than ever to react, to react quickly, have opinions, to have opinions about nearly everything, and to jump to conclusions. Indeed, much in our connected Webworld encourages us to have those characteristics, to be that way, and to behave in those ways.[34]

One of the great temptations in life is to allow ourselves to get sidetracked; sidetracked from who we really are and from what we really hope to accomplish. I'm convinced that a major reason for Jesus' prayer-saturated life was his desire to remain focused on his mission. The initial temptation (Matthew 4:1-11) was all about altering his course and becoming the popular Messiah who could easily be recognized as such by the people. The temptations to be a bread Messiah ("to use his powers selfishly and for his own use"), a spectacular wonder-working Messiah ("to seek to attract people to him by providing them with sensations"), and a political Messiah who would overthrow Roman domination ("the temptation to try

---

34 Brian T. Watson, *Headed Into the Abyss* (Swampscott, Massachusetts: Anvilside Press, 2019), 4.

to advance by retreating, to try to change the world by becoming like the world"),[35] were always lurking in the shadows.

Getting caught up in the hyper-present means responding to the questions, demands, and temptations of life with quick reactions and almost immediate conclusions in a world that wants our responses right now. Jesus' prayer life kept him on course as the Messiah the Father had sent him to be. Questions from the Pharisees constantly challenged his methods and his very way of life with his disciples. "*Is it lawful to give tribute to Caesar?*" (Mark 12:14) was a question that received a surprising well-thought-out answer from Jesus that, according to the text, amazed even the Pharisees. It was really an open-door answer. Jesus asked for a Roman coin, asked whose picture and title were on it, and then said, "*Well then, give to Caesar what belongs to him. But everything that belongs to God must be given to God*" (Mark 12:17). The work of deciding who was to get what was left to the Pharisees to decide.

The best response to a frequently asked question of seniors "How are you?" was intended to be humorous but carried a weighty wisdom. The reply to "How are you? was a thoughtful, "How soon do you have to know?" Only when you are in your eighties do you understand that reply. But the application does not end with matters of aging. Too many of the questions that come to us in life have a context of ambiguity that would take a lifetime to unravel. Why do we feel we have to immediately respond when someone asks us a question? My dad's frequent response to one of my questions was, "Let me mull that over." So much of Webworld is so shallow because so much of it is "off the cuff." Jesus was not an "off the cuff" Messiah. The silent years of his life (from 12 to about 30) were years of Torah study, prayer, meditation, and conversation with the rabbis. The wisdom of Jesus' stories, teachings, and life came from thought-out purpose and long-range strategies.

---

35 William Barclay, *The Gospel of Matthew*, Vol. 1 (Philadelphia: Westminster, 1958), 60-64.

A Verse to Remember

Psalm 84:11 – *For the Lord God is our light and protector. He gives us grace and glory.*

Chapter Six:

Is God in the Hedge Business?

The Biblical Foundation

The Disturbing Book of Job

> *One day the angels came to present themselves before the Lord and Satan also came with them. The Lord said to Satan, "Where have you come from?"*
>
> *Satan answered the Lord, "From roaming through the earth and going back and forth in it."*
>
> *Then the Lord said to Satan, "Have you considered my servant Job? There is no one on earth like him; he is blameless and upright, a man who fears God and shuns evil."*
>
> *"Does Job serve God for nothing?" Satan replied. "Have you not put a hedge around him and his household and everything he has? You have blessed the work of his hands, so that his flocks and herds are spread throughout the land. But now stretch out your hand and strike everything he has, and he will surely curse you to your face."* (Job 1:6-11 TNIV).

I begin with an ancient Greek dialogue from the delightful book Plato and a Platypus Walk into a Bar:[36]

> Dimitri: If Atlas holds up the world, what holds up Atlas?
> Tasso: Atlas stands on the back of a turtle.
> Dimitri: But what does the turtle stand on?
> Tasso: Another turtle.
> Dimitri: And what does that turtle stand on?
> Tasso: My dear Dimitri, it's turtles all the way down!

---

36 Thomas Cathcart and Daniel Klein, *Plato and a Platypus Walk into a Bar* (New York: Abrams Image, 2007), 1

And then the authors' comment: "That's the way it is with philosophy and philosophers: It's questions all the way down." [37] That's just about the way we feel when we begin to look at the book of Job and the way it begins. We are told about a good and great man named Job and suddenly the scene shifts to a heavenly council meeting where God is getting reports from his scouts. The answer to the question in Job 1:7, From where have you come? Is "Doing my job of checking out things." And then comes the contest. Job knows nothing about this meeting (and never finds out!). My take on this is: in the heavenly council meetings, just hope your name never comes up!

From Harold Kushner's excellent book *When Bad Things Happen to a Good Person*:[38]

> Job is part of the Hebrew Bible known as miscellaneous writings. The three major writings in his group, Psalms, Proverbs, and Job are sometimes referred to a "books of truth," referring to the spiritual truths of the Psalms, the practical truths of Proverbs, and the philosophical-theological insights of Job. (Note: The book of Job, along with Psalms, Proverbs, Ecclesiastes, and the Song of Song, is classified as one of the Wisdom books.)
>
> There are really two books of Job: the fable of Job, a very old folktale (chapters 1, 2, and 42) and then the poem of Job, a much later, more complicated work. The author of the poem totally leaves the fable behind.

Katherine Dell suggests that the theological problems in the book of Job concern three major issues:[39]

1. Disinterested righteousness: "Does Job fear God for nothing?"

---

37 Ibid, 4.
38 Harold Kushner, *When Bad Things Happen to a Good Person* (New York: Schocken Books, 2012), 15, 41.
39 Gail R. O'Day and David L. Peterson, eds., *Theological Bible Commentary* (Louisville: Westminster John Knox Press, 2009), 167-168.

2. The doctrine of retribution. The question here is whether those who are righteous are indeed rewarded by God in this life and whether those who behave in wicked fashion are punished.
3. The relationship between God and human beings. Can human beings have a relationship with a God who seemingly dispenses justice as he wills and who does not appear to be restricted by human ideas of justice?

In *The Mercer Commentary on the Old Testament*, Samuel E. Balentine states what I believe to be the central problem in dealing with the book of Job:[40]

> It is remarkable that despite the universal sympathy with this book, so little of the complexity and the candor of Job's engagement with God is appropriated by the community of faith. Too often the message of the book is reduced to a conventional slogan: the patience of Job (cf. James 5:11). As with all slogans, this one distorts by oversimplifying. The full picture of Job and the God before whom he presents his case is both more demanding and more honest.

The Question at Issue is Often Overlooked

The question raised in the prologue by Satan (actually "The Satan" which is not a proper name but a title) appears to be the central issue: "*Does Job serve God for nothing?*" In response to God's commendation of Job, Satan replies that the only reason for his spotless service is that it has paid off in incredible wealth. Satan contends that if Job loses these blessings, he will turn his back on God. The reason Job is faithful is that goodness pays dividends. Then Satan gives his reason for Job's faithfulness: "You have put a protective hedge around Job and everything he has." That is the reason for the chapter's title: "Is God in the Hedge Business?"

The contest that follows Satan's challenge results in Job's losing everything he has and everyone he loves. He is ultimately reduced

---

40 Watson E. Mills and Richard F. Wilson, eds., *The Mercer Commentary on the Old Testament* (Macon: Mercer University Press, 2003), 405.

to a mass of ulcers, sitting on a trash heap. It is from this trash heap that Job speaks his wisdom and his three friends offer their relentless defense of God. Their defense is based on the current belief that suffering is the result of sin. Job is suffering; he must have sinned. Job continues to proclaim his innocence and the injustice of his suffering.

We will examine some biblical texts, but I begin with the observation that, if you live long enough with open eyes, it does not take very long to observe how frequently bad things happen to good people or, more accurately, bad things happen to all people and, more often than not, there is no apparent relation to how one's life has been lived. *"(God) gives his sunlight to both the evil and the good, and he sends rain on the just and on the unjust, too"* (Matthew 5:45). James 4:13-14 suggests that "things just happen": *Look here, you people who say, "Today or tomorrow we are going to a certain town and will stay there a year. We will do business there and make a profit." How do you know what will happen tomorrow?*

In John 16:33 Jesus tells his disciples something none of them wanted to hear: *"Here on earth you will have many trials and sorrows. But take heart, because I have overcome the world."* Paul must have said a hearty "Amen!" as he wrote to the Corinthians defending himself against false apostles: *"I have worked harder, been put in jail more often, been whipped times without number, and faced death again and again. Five different times the Jews gave me thirty-nine lashes. Three times I was beaten with rods. Once I was stoned. Three times I was shipwrecked. Once I spent a whole night and a day adrift at sea. I have traveled many weary miles"* (2 Corinthians 10:23-26). If God is in the hedge business, some guardian angel was asleep at the switch.

There are times when all of us have felt that we were spared from some catastrophic situation. But there is no justification (or Scriptures) for the belief that if one has faith in God and leads a good life that God will keep the bad things in the world from happening. Paul maintains in Romans 8:22 that *all creation has been groaning as in the pains of childbirth right up to the present time.* Meaning: this remains an unfinished creation. I Corinthians 15 is Paul's great chapter on Resurrection and in verse 22 he writes that "*the last enemy to be destroyed is death.*" Death is not only our enemy, it is also God's enemy. Everything is not yet as God intends. That will come with the new heaven and the new earth described in Revelation 21:4 – *(God) will remove all of their sorrows, and there will be no more death or sorrows or crying or pain. For the old world and its evils are gone forever.*"

The Psalms are filled with cries for deliverance and rescue. The question "Why?" has been the one consistent cry of humanity since the beginning of existence. To my favorite triad of mystery, paradox, and ambiguity, I should probably add "complexity" as Samuel Ballentine does in his reading of Job. There are no simple answers to the problems of evil and suffering in the world because they bring with them no easy questions. I have often wondered if we take seriously Jesus' response to his disciples' question in John 9:2 – "*Rabbi, who sinned, this man or his parents, that he was born blind?*" (TNIV). Jesus' answer, *"Neither,"* meant this is not the way the world works. It is not that simple. Theodicy will forever remain the big issue: God is good, loving, and omnipotent but terrible things continue to happen to his children.

Does Job Have Anything to Say to Us Today?

Someone wrote on a pre-title page of *Answer to Job* by C. G. Jung[41] "It is a job to understand Job!" This is one of many times I have found valuable observations in a used book. It may be a job to understand Job but it is worth the effort. After reading the book, an editorial note seems like an understatement: "He was fully aware of the controversial character of his ideas and of the hostility it was bound to waken."[42] Jung confesses: "I cannot, therefore, write in a coolly objective manner, but must allow my emotional subjectivity to speak if I want to describe what I feel when I read certain books of the Bible, or when I remember the impressions I have received

---
41 C. G. Jung, *Answer to Job* (Princeton: Princeton University Press, 1958).
42 Ibid, v.

from the doctrines of our faith."[43] My contention is that, understood for the type of literature it represents and the purposes of such writings, the book of Job provides a treasure trove of material for soul-searching and wider discussions about the great issues of life and faith. I am so grateful it was included in the Bible as one of those books that brings to our attention matters that refuse to go unnoticed.

One of my recommendations for reading, meditation, and discussion is *Consider My Servant Job* by Paul Ciholas.[44] "He brings understanding and exegetical skills to Job that provide insight, meaning, guidance, and encouragement to those who are asking 'Why me?'" (back cover). "On her deathbed, Gertrude Stein is said to have asked, 'What is the answer?' Then after a long silence, 'What is the question?'... We tend to lose track of the questions about things that matter always, life-and-death questions about meaning, purpose, and value. To lose track of such deep questions as these is to risk losing track of who we really are in our own depths and where we are really going."[45] Job forces us to ask some of the central questions of our own lives.

Paul Ciholas introduces his book by recounting the Palm Sunday tornado of 1994 that destroyed the building of the Goshen United Methodist Church in Piedmont, Alabama, killing 20 people and injuring others. The pastor, the Rev. Kelly Clem, lost her four-year-old daughter, Hannah. To people around her who groped for an explanation, she responded, "We do not know why. I do not think 'why' is the question right now. We just have to help each other through it."[46] Following this story is the line: "With God we always stand at the door of the unknown."[47]

---

43 Ibid, xv.
44 Paul Ciholas, *Consider My Servant Job* (Peabody, Mass: Hendrickson Publishers, 1998).
45 Frederick Buechner, *Listening to Your Life* (New York: HarperSanFrancisco, 1992), 124.
46 Paul Ciholas, *Consider My Servant Job,* 15.
47 Ibid, 16.

A line from the book that continues to demand my attention is: "Perhaps we are destined to find God when he no longer makes sense to us, when he transcends all of what we can say, think, or believe about him."[48] That appears to be what happened to Job.

Some Ramifications

Logic in One Direction

> (Le Fleur) had been a believer earlier in his life, and the day Lilly was born, he did feel blessed by something larger than all of them…But after her death, he viewed things differently. God? Why turn to God now? (He was part of a group of shipwrecked survivors in a raft.) Where was God when his mother-in-law fell asleep in her beach chair? Where was God when his daughter got swept out to sea? Why didn't God just make her little feet run the other way, back to safety, back to the house, back to her mother and her father? What kind of a God lets a child die that way?…Why not pin Him down? Hold his accountable for all the horrors He allowed in the world? Le Fleur would have.[49]

Le Fleur reaches the same logical conclusion many others have reached. If God is omnipotent (which is the major thesis of most theologies) and can do anything he wills to do, why doesn't he activate that power and put an end to all the tragedies, suffering, and misery in the world? If he does it some of the time, why can't he do it all the time? Why not hold God accountable for all the horrors he has allowed in the world? If God can do something about the horrors and doesn't do anything, it is the logical conclusion that the buck stops with him.

In a world of either/or simplicity, that appears to be the conclusion thinking people come to. (The New Atheists in our time have solved the "problem" of evil with this kind of logic.) You don't have to be in a lifeboat on the open sea to do this kind of

---
48 Ibid, 51.
49 Mitch Albom, *The Stranger in the Boat* (New York: Harper, 2021), 201.

thinking. When the tragedies of life just keep rolling in like the tide, you wonder why the only one who can stop them chooses to do nothing. Mitch Albom explores this "mystery" in the form of a story that will keep you immersed in its unfolding. The stranger in the lifeboat doesn't so much give answers as different perspectives and new questions.

"If I ruled the world" is a theme that has been played out in various ways. In the various scenarios, the one who is given the rulership always concludes that he/she would create a perfect world without any pain, suffering, or evil. Life would be "just a bowl of cherries." They never tell us exactly how they would remove all the pits, but a "pit-less" world is what they promise. Few of the difficult issues that form the context of our world are addressed: freedom of will, human desires and drives, the competition of the marketplace, definitions and boundaries of leadership, supervision and control when things go wrong, and the big one – WHO will be in charge and enforce this perfection? (It is assumed that in a perfect world everyone would automatically do the right thing. History does not validate this assumption).

Le Fleur's is simply logic that ignores so many other impinging factors.

An Answer Rejected in Job But Not in Modern Culture

> Cherish sat up a bit straighter against her pillows and sniffled. "Oh, I know I'm not makin' much sense. But they say bad things happen to bad people, and I think everyone would agree that miscarriages and premature babies aren't exactly good news. So the way things have gone for me, I sometimes wonder if I'm being punished for something. Do you think that is possible?"
>
> Novie grasped Cherish's hand again, this time more firmly. "I most certainly do not, young lady. I don't know why you would even get a notion like that into your head. This is a challenge you've been given for whatever reasons, and you

and Henry will just have to be strong enough to work your way through it."[50]

The ever present "they" are always saying something that varies dramatically with circumstance, time, and culture. In the book of Job, "they" (the three friends) are so persistent, that God has to show up and tell them that they are wrong: Job's sufferings are not the result of any sin on his part. We have dealt with Jesus' answer to the question about the reason for a man's being born blind. His contention is that it is not the result of anybody's sin (John 9:1-5). The condition only provides Jesus' opportunity to demonstrate the grace of God (he then proceeds to give the gift of sight).

As in the quote from the above novel, I have heard far too many ask, "What have I done to deserve this?" Most of the time, nobody deserves what they are going through. A coffee mug quote I spotted years ago read: "Life isn't fair, so it doesn't make sense." One of the reasons for the continuing assertion that the bad things that happen to people are the result of sin is an attempt to make sense of life. To make it reasonable. To make it understandable. Dare I suggest that frequently life is neither reasonable nor understandable.

The late John Claypool lost a 9 ½ year old daughter to leukemia and preached a series of sermons to his people at Crescent Hill Baptist Church in Louisville about his experience. He put them in a book titled "*Tracks of a Fellow Struggler.*" Here is an excerpt:

> The thing I have to share may surprise you a bit, but I must in all honesty confess it, and that is: I have found no answers to the deepest questions of this experience. Why do little girls get leukemia? Why is there leukemia at all?[51]

Claypool may not give answers but his gives this insight: "The Bible arranges life and thought in just (this) sequence – the challenge to go on living even though I have no answer or any complete

---

50 Robert Dalby, *A Piggly Wiggly Christmas* (New York: G. P. Putnam's Sons, 2010), 168-169.
51 John Claypool, *Tracks of a Fellow Struggler* (Waco: Word Books, 1974), 27.

explanation…If we…try to put understanding before the living of life, everything freezes and we become immobilized."[52]

"It's Such a Bitter Pill to Take"

(A phrase from a song in *Mary Poppins*)

> "I know nothing of your brother. Nothing at all about the child you grew up with."
> "I was younger, and I looked up to him. I thought he was absolutely wonderful. And he was. All the girls at my school adored him. But he had a fatal flaw. My father never saw it, but I did. Because he was always popular and everyone praised everything he did, he never had to develop character. And when the world no longer lifted him on its shoulders and called him wonderful, he didn't know how to cope with adversity."[53]

Where and how do we learn the great lessons and survival skills of life? Where do we learn how to cope with adversity? Most would agree it is not when the crowd is cheering us on and we are basking in the blessings and achievements of life. One of the most difficult texts to probe is Hebrews 5:8-8: *So even though Jesus was God's Son, he learned obedience from the things he suffered. In this way, God qualified him as a perfect High Priest, and he became the source of eternal salvation for all who obey him.* It would take another book and the skill of a theologian far better than I am to fully explore the depths and dimensions of these words. The obvious and clear meaning is: Jesus' suffering completed his understanding and compassion for the human condition. He does not stand apart from his suffereing, he stands with us in every way. Who else is better qualified to be our High Priest?

When we are introduced to Joseph in the Genesis saga, he can easily be perceived as a spoiled tattle-tale. He is the father's favorite of the twelve sons, and with the father's gift of his executive coat, he relates to them as their superior supervisor. When we read about

---

52 Ibid, 28.
53 Charles Todd, *The Black Ascot* (New York: William Morrow, 2019), 121-122.

Joseph at the conclusion of the story, we wonder how this can be the same person we encountered earlier. What transformed him? Not continued affirmation and adulation, but a pit, the journey to Egypt as a slave, his role as a servant, and his experience in prison. There are no angelic encouragements or special revelations. The occurring phrase throughout the story is simply: *and the Lord was with Joseph* (Genesis 39:2).

David Heller, in *Just Build the Ark and the Animals Will Come*, provides interviews with children on their take about many of the familiar Bible stories. To the question:

> Because the coat made them so jealous, what did the other sons of Jacob do to young Joseph?" Keith age 11 answered, "They sold him to Pharaoh's servants for something like fifty bucks and one of those sundial watches." Dean, age 10 said, "They threw him down a well to see if he would bounce… Joseph didn't bounce."[54]

Dean misses the point of the Joseph saga in the Bible: Joseph does bounce! He keeps bouncing back. That is the secret of his perseverance. Joseph gets right back up every time he falls down or is pushed down. Each time he bounces back he is a better person, more compassionate, more understanding, more committed to achieve God's purpose for him. Joseph could never suddenly have been transported from his role as brother supervisor to supervisor of crop production in Egypt. His journey was slow and difficult, but one in which he learned in every situation to give his best to whatever role he was assigned. He, too, learned obedience from the things he suffered. Was there another way? I doubt it. Is there another way for us? Speaking for myself only: I doubt it.

---

54 David Heller, *Just Build the Ark and the Animals Will Come* (New York: Villard Books, 1994), 58.

A Verse to Remember

Psalm 40:12 – *For troubles surround me – too many to count! They pile up so high I can't see my way out. They are more numerous than the hairs on my head. I have lost all my courage.*

Chapter Seven:

The Danger of Unrealistic Expectations

The Biblical Foundation

A Time of Courage and Faith

> *"All of you will desert me," Jesus told them. "For the Scriptures say, 'God will strike the Shepherd, and the sheep will be scattered.' But after I am raised from the dead, I will go ahead of you to Galilee and meet you there."*
> *Peter said to him, "Even if everyone else deserts you, I never will."*
> *"Peter," Jesus replied, "the truth is, this very night, before the rooster crows twice, you will deny me three times."*
> *"No!" Peter insisted. "Not even if I have to die with you! I will never deny you!" And all the others vowed the same."*
> (Mark 14:27-31).

> *"Simon, Simon, Satan has asked to have all of you, to sift you like wheat. But I have pleaded in prayer for you, Simon, that your faith should not fail. So when you have repented and turned to me again, strengthen and build up your brothers"* (Luke 22: 31-34).

There is no doubt that this group of disciples (minus Judas) believed they were on the winning team. They had seen and heard too much to believe otherwise. The Kingdom was about to dawn and the land of Israel was about to be set free from the heavy boots of Roman oppression. Wasn't the Triumphal Entry an indication that Jesus was about to make his final move? In looking back, we understand that what most refer to as Palm Sunday is better termed Passion Sunday. It was not the beginning of the end as it appeared the following Friday, but the beginning of the beginning as the next Sunday morning revealed.

The reason for my believing in the optimism of the disciples even in Jesus words over the bread and the cup at the Supper, is that there is every indication they were prepared to assume places of honor and power when Jesus took over. James and John had already asked for places on Jesus' right and left hand when he took his place on his throne, and, according to Luke (22:24-30), on the way to the Upper Room the disciples were arguing over which of them was the greatest. They were certain Jesus was the long-awaited Messiah and they were just the courageous bunch to bring in the Kingdom. If they met danger on the Mount of Olives, they were ready. They announced to Jesus, "We have two swords among us." Jesus replied, "That's enough," but they certainly did not grasp the meaning of those words (Luke 22:38).

Troops usually march to war with a parade, bands playing, and people cheering. That is how it is before a battle. In a recent WWI movie, two men in a trench are sharing their insights into what they have experienced so far in combat. One finally confesses, "This is not what I expected." When the music has faded and the cheering crowd has gone home, the horrors of a war like none had ever seen became the only reality. The disciples had no idea what they were getting into. When the mob arrived with the leading priests and captains of the Temple guard, the disciples ask, *"Lord, should we fight? We brought the swords!" And one of them slashed at the high priest's servant and cut off his right ear. But Jesus said, "Don't resist anymore." And he touched the place where the man's ear had been and healed him* (Luke 22:49-51).

What follows is arrest, Peter's denials, and a hasty exit by the other disciples. (The beloved disciple in John 19:26 is another issue recorded only in this Gospel). What we do know is that on Sunday morning we find the disciples in hiding for fear of the Roman authorities. When the women who went to the tomb report to the disciples what happened, *the story sounded like nonsense, so they didn't believe it*" (Luke 24:11). Bravery returns only after they encounter the risen Lord for themselves.

It's Often Difficult to Realize How Vulnerable We Are

Peter was a seasoned fisherman who felt he was ready for anything. His life was not spent on the safety of the bank, baiting a hook, and reeling in the fish. In a small fishing boat, he and his partners worked with heavy nets often in the middle of heavy seas. The Sea of Galilee was known for severe storms that gave little advance warning. He had successfully braved many of those and probably felt he was ready for anything. He was certainly no coward. But he had never faced an angry mob of religious enthusiasts empowered by Roman swords. He didn't know how he would feel until he got there. It certainly was not what he expected.

With Peter's boasting of remaining faithful even if everyone else turned away, was the expression of a false confidence that he could handle anything that came his way. He had no idea what was coming. Bravado before the crisis is no indication of what will happen, or how one will feel, when everything breaks loose. Even Jesus prepared himself with honest, soul-searching prayers, and honest confession of how difficult the coming challenge was going to be for him. This was no simple, "It's the Father's will, so I'll just do it." Luke describes Gethsemane's praying like this: *He prayed more fervently, and he was in such agony of spirit that his sweat fell to the ground like great drops of blood* (22:44).

Jesus knew what was coming and he knew what he had to be prepared for. He knew how difficult it was going to be to maintain his composure and follow through in the events that were unfolding. Jesus asked, that, if possible, this cup of suffering would be taken from him (Luke 22:42). Big question: could Jesus have refused to drink of that cup? If Jesus really did share his humanity with us, then the answer has to be "Yes". The temptation experience recorded in Matthew 4:1-11 appears to be focused on the kind of Messiah Jesus is going to be. The temptation is to assume the popular role of Messiah which included the overthrow of Rome and the restoration of the nation of Israel. Jesus and the tempter cite different Scriptures to defend two different messianic roles. A temptation always offers another possibility and Jesus refused that possibility. It is reaffirmed many times and for the final time in Gethsemane.

A Powerful Force of Evil is at Work in the World

Much has been written and argued about the origin, nature, and purpose of Satan. The word in both Hebrew and Christian Scripture means "the Adversary". Pictured as the opponent, challenger, and rival of both God and humans, two Scriptures speak to the power and determination of this adversary. Luke 22:31-34, cited at the beginning of this chapter, begins with the repetition of Peter's name, "Simon, Simon," which adds weight to the warning.

The threat of "sifting him like wheat" can be compared with the picture in I Peter 5:8 – *Be careful! Watch out for attacks from the Devil, your great enemy. He prowls around like a roaring lion, looking for some victim to devour.* Being sifted like wheat or devoured by a lion are both meant to alert us to the dangers and destructive possibilities of underestimating the dangers in this world and overestimating our own defenses. Jesus indicates that it is only his prayers that prevent Peter's witness and ministry from being destroyed.

What will enable Peter to "strengthen and encourage" his brothers, is that, after his denials, he will be more aware of his arrogance and his vulnerability. After his failure, he will find himself standing on level ground with the other disciples. He will no longer have the high ground of superiority (which, of course, he never really had to begin with). Whatever you do with this wheat sifter and roaring lion, we need to heed the call to "Be careful and watch out!" Ephesians 6:11 gives this advice: Be strong with the Lord's mighty power. Put on all of God's armor so that you will be able to stand firm against all strategies and tricks of the Devil. The pieces of this armor indicate a spiritual warfare: (13-18): the belt of truth, the body armor of God's righteousness, the shoes of peace that comes from the Good News (Gospel), the shield of faith, the helmet of salvation, and the sword of the Spirit (the word of God).

There is an addition to the pieces of armor: *Pray at all times and on every occasion in the power of the Holy Spirit. Stay alert and be persistent in your prayers for all Christians everywhere.* This parallels I Thessalonians 5:17 – *pray continually* (TNIV). A period of Scripture reading, prayer, and meditation in the morning sets the stage for sentence prayers throughout the day. When I was about to enter a hospital room for an uncertain visit, I would often pray: "Lord, I'm not certain what I'm going to find behind this door. Help me to meet _____ where and how she is and be pastoral in all I do." When waiting for one of my critics to arrive at the office, "Lord, let me receptive to what I need to hear and not shift to the defensive." What entering a Deacons' meeting where some challenging issues were up for discussion, "Lord, as always, it is the leadership of your Spirit that we are all seeking. May we be listeners and appropriate responders." These kinds of prayers can be offered anywhere throughout the day and make a difference in how well we feel prepared to deal with what is coming. Sometimes with a schedule of a large number of hospital visits, I would take a coffee break in mid-afternoon and offer these silent words: "Thank you, Lord, for this time of rest, reflection, and refreshment. May I be prepared for effective ministry as a result of these moments."

I would like to tell you that in over sixty years of ministry I never felt sifted or almost devoured. On certain days, my fully human spirituality became simply super fully human. Not much spirituality was in evidence. Not every day found me at my best. Every effort was made to learn what I could from those days, and, like Peter, be equipped the next day for strengthening and building up others.

Some Ramifications

A Common Experience

> Jack (C. S. Lewis) was in WWI: The cold, the wet mud, the marching; it was what Jack had prepared for during his training, yet he was completely unprepared for the reality.[55]

Sidebar: much of the following has changed for the better but the following describes the period of my earlier days of ministry. Warning: this section is highly personal and confessional.

Three years of seminary training and a further two years in securing my D. Min (Doctor of Ministry) were meant to prepare me for ministry with a local congregation. I had stumbled awkwardly in six years of student pastorates but was certain a "real" full-time position was going to be another matter. The reality was somewhat different as Jack Lewis experienced when he hit the trenches. "They're firing real bullets!" must have been his first shock. There are days when I felt the same kind of shock. The professors and classmates were not present to encourage and offer guidance. The awareness of what could (and did) go wrong and the consequences of false steps or miscalculations loomed large. I don't know why I didn't take Scott Peck's opening three words in his classic *The Road Less Traveled* to heart: "Life is difficult."[56] There are always difficulties in any occupation, any endeavor, any effort to accomplish whatever, and any goal we seek to attain. It is simply the nature of life – all of life. Peter was naïve to think he was an exceptional disciple; I was naïve to think I was an exceptional minister.

It is not an exaggeration to contend that when my formal education ended my real in-the-field education began. Most of the people with whom I worked were just as I had imagined they would be. However, some had models of ideal pastors based on someone who had preceded me. The expectations did not match

---

[55] Patti Callahan, *Once Upon a Wardrobe* (New York: Harper Muse, 2021), 235.
[56] Scott Peck, *The Road Less Traveled* (New York: Touchstone, 1978), 15.

what I could deliver both because of my inexperience and because my gifts did not match those of the predecessor. Unrealistic expectations (as far as I was concerned) ruled the day. My wife was hit by the traditional role model of a minister's wife that was basically an unsalaried full-time church employee in all but title.

As my spirituality was fully human, so my role as a pastor was fully-human. Most accepted that, but a few believed a "man of the cloth" was a different creature. I knew the best I could ever hope to be was fully human in whatever role I assumed. One of my major flaws was that I tended to take criticism personally. I had a whole shelf of Alban Institute materials about church organization, planning, and keys to relating to church leadership. I had a lot of theory that never made it down into the day-to-day conflicts that are always part of any organization – secular or religious.

It didn't help that I began in the days when the minister was expected to deliver a sermon on Sunday morning and Sunday night, plus present an in-depth Bible study every Wednesday night. That was in addition to visitation of every member who was in the hospital, those in nursing homes, and keeping in touch with the homebound. Throw in pastoral counseling, meetings of every shape and description, and being held accountable for church attendance and financial stability. Most ministers I knew worked at least fifty to sixty hours each week.

The bottom line is that I had read about the challenges but never knew what they were like until I met them face to face.

It was naïve to believe that I was going to be everyone's ministerial cup of tea. It was naïve to believe that I was going to be loved by everyone in the congregation or that there would be no honest and sincere opposition to things I brought up for consideration. Ministers, as well as most caregivers, are known as people pleasers. If you mean anywhere close to one-hundred percent, that is an unachievable goal. The old rule that made the rounds in my early days was: When you begin a new pastorate you can count on three things: ten percent of the people will think you are the best pastor they have ever had; ten percent of the people will wonder where the call committee got your name; the other eighty percent will work with you and appreciate your efforts if they believe you care about them and are working at the job. The advice that came with that prediction: thank the Lord for the ten percent at the top, concentrate your efforts on the eighty percent in the middle, and pray that God will give you guidance and grace for dealing with the ten percent at the bottom. It turned out to be pretty much that way. My big mistake was to be like Peter and assume strength and gifts and capabilities I did not possess and unrealistic expectations of what ministry was like.

My biggest regret is that I did not have a spiritual director from the beginning with whom I could meet on a regular basis to get some feedback on how I was doing as a human being and as a minister. I needed someone to help me be aware of my strengths and weaknesses, my blind spots, and my assumptions that clouded realistic assessments. I am grateful for those who, along the way, periodically came to my rescue with the guidance and wisdom I did not possess.

It's Unthinkable

> *Look here, you people who say, "Today or tomorrow we are going to a certain town and will stay there a year. We will do business there and make a profit." How do you know what will happen tomorrow? For you your life is like the morning fog – it's here a little while, then it's gone. What you ought to say is, "If the Lord wants us to, we will live and do this or that."* (James 4:13-15).

I suspect that not many sermons have been preached on the above text; it is not something that makes for very "good news" in a Sunday morning worship service. Since it is a part of the biblical canon, it needs to be placed along with those verses that promise God's protection, guidance, and safe conduct. It is one of those "on the other hand" verses that keep the mystery, paradox, and ambiguity of faith alive and well.

Peter's, "I would never deny you," is the confidence of one who "knows" something that is unthinkable. The classic modern illustration of such thinking comes from the survivors of the Titanic. Andrew Wilson has assembled interviews and writings from many of those survivors; it all makes for compelling and instructive reading:

> Sylvia Caldwell, who was travelling second class with her husband, Albert, and ten-month-old son, Alden remembered asking a deckhand who was carrying luggage on board whether the vessel really was unsinkable. The man turned to her and said, "God himself could not sink this ship."[57]

Less shocking but illustrative of the self-confidence on board and of the era in general is the story of Jack Thayer, an American who had been visiting Europe with his parents.

> That Sunday in April 1912, Jack could see his future mapped out as plain as the clear, straight line of the distant horizon. After graduating from the Haverford School outside Philadelphia, he would attend Princeton, then travel to Europe, returning home to America to practice private of commercial banking. As he said, "It could be planned. It was planned it was a certainty."[58]

Something else was also an unrecognized certainty. "Titanic was carrying 2,228 people, yet her sixteen lifeboats (plus four Englehardt collapsibles) provided enough space for only 1,178. Loss of life would be inevitable."[59] No one on the ship took into account the possibility that an iceberg could change "unthinkable" to "a real possibility." I'm not sure just how Peter could have equipped himself to overcome the temptations of denial, I do know many of the measures that could have been taken on the Titanic if there had been the assumption that sinking was a possibility. "It could never

---

57 Andrew Wilson, *Shadow of the Titanic,* 18-19.
58 Ibid, 20.
59 Ibid, 42.

happen here," has been the lament of many who later experienced the happening of the unthinkable.

How we live our lives, equip our days, set our priorities, and structure our schedules depends a great deal on how we number our days. This phrase has come to us in the KJV of Psalm 90:12 – *So teach us to number our days, that we may apply our hearts to wisdom.* For the modern reader, I believe the meaning is better captured by the NLT: *Teach us to make the most of our time, so that we may grow in wisdom.* When we see life as a gift and time on loan, the wisdom of this perspective shapes how we spend our time. It is not the call to live in fear but in the confidence of the one who tells us: *"Don't be troubled. You trust in God, now trust in me"* (John 14:1). Even if we are on the Titanic? Yes.

Despair or Redemptive Action?

When the unthinkable happens, what are you going to do? In the face of his denials, Peter's over-confidence did not signal the end of his usefulness, but the beginning. Jesus' words to Peter give the prescription following the unthinkable: *"So when you have repented and turned to me again, strengthen and build up your brothers"* (Luke 22:32). The old Peter could not have done this; this new fully human disciple could. He would not be speaking down to his brothers, but as one of them – in every way.

Here is another less dramatic, but highly practical, illustration:

> (Lou) thought back to the time when (his daughter Emily's) computer crashed, and with it the term paper she had finished less than a day before. There were no tears. No throwing things. No rants. She did not talk about asking for an extension. What she did instead was to berate herself for not making a backup, then vowed never to repeat the mistake again. Finally, after a bowl of her favorite mint chocolate chip ice cream, she gathered her reference books and reworked the entire eleven-page paper in one marathon session.[60]

---

60 Michael Palmer, *Resistant* (New York: St. Martin's Press, 2014), 124-125.

That is what we do when our expectations come crashing down because of something that was unforeseen. We grieve what we have to grieve, learn what could have been done differently, and set about to accomplish what has to be done in light of what is. So many times in life and in my ministry, it was necessary to say, "Here is the situation. Here is what I believe needs to be done. Here is the way I'm going to begin." Redemptive action is always better than ten tons of regret. As a new reality dawns, it is time for a new awakening. Like Peter, there is always the promise that things we never dreamed we could do become possible because we now stand on the other side of the unthinkable. No unthinkable needs to be the end; it always holds the promise of things that were not even seen before.

A Verse to Remember

Psalm 57:10 – *For your unfailing love is as high as the heavens. Your faithfulness reaches to the clouds.*

Chapter Eight:

In the Here and Now of Life's Specificity

The Biblical Foundation

How Did Jesus Develop His Daily Agenda?

Send out your light and your truth; let them guide me (Psalm 43:3).

As Jesus walked beside the Sea of Galilee, he saw Simon and his brother Andrew casting a net into the lake… When he had gone a little further he saw James son of Zebedee and his brother John in a boat (Mark 1:16, 19).

A man with leprosy came to him and begged him on his knees, "If you are willing, you can make me clean" (Mark 1:40).

Once again Jesus went out beside the lake. A large crowd came to him, and he began to teach them (Mark 2:13).

Another time Jesus went into the synagogue, and a man with a shriveled hand was there (Mark 3:1).

That day when evening came, he said to his disciples, "Let us go over to the other side." Leaving the crowd behind, they took him along, just as he was, in the boat (Mark 4:35).

Then Jesus said, "Let's get away from the crowds for a while and rest" (Mark 6:31).

When Jesus got out of the boat, a man with an evil spirit came from the tombs to meet him (Mark 5:2).

It is difficult for me to imagine Jesus, in prayer, with a "Today" do list in one hand on which he has written: "Heal a blind man. Cure two lepers. Respond to questions from a Pharisee." There is no doubt on the Sabbath he would be planning to go to the Synagogue, usually to teach. There might be other specifics that were obvious for the day, but I believe that most of his time (frequently all night) was spent getting himself ready for whatever demands the day brought.

It appears that the Gospel writers gathered a group of pericopes about Jesus and arranged them. Such phrases in the NJB as: *It happened one Sabbath day* (Mk 2:23); *Another time he went to the Synagogue* (Mk 3:1); *He went home again* (Mk 3:20); *Again he began to teach by the lakeside* (Mk 4:1*)*; *He made his tour around the villages, teaching* (Mk 6:7*)*; *And now once again a great crowd had gathered* (Mk 8:1); *People were bringing their little children to him* (Mk 10:13); *James and John, the sons of Zebedee, approached him* (Mk 10:35); *They came to Jerusalem again* (Mk 11:27); *While teaching in the Temple, Jesus said* (Mk 12:38). As a day unfolded, Jesus encountered opportunities for ministry and witness and he was ready.

As Jesus used his prayer book, one of his key verses must have been Psalm 43:3 –*Send out your light and truth, let them guide me.* Light and truth are great guiding principles that, once in place, help us see what we need to see and bring guidance, direction, and, in the case of Jesus, healing and restoration. When our lives are filled with the fruit of the Spirit (Gal. 5:22): *love, joy, peace, patience, kindness, goodness, faithfulness, gentleness, and self-control,* we are more likely to be able to meet the various demanding situations that fill our day. We can't know in advance many of the challenges that wait for us each day, so how can we possibly get ready for each situation? We can prepare ourselves. On days when my stock of spiritual fruit was low, I experienced much more frustration and failure, even when I was able to pull a few tricks of the trade out of my pastoral care hat. How I *was* had a lot to do with how I *did*.

I don't believe that when Jesus got into the boat with the disciples (Mk 4:35), he thought to himself, "The disciples will never forget what I am about to do!" He was exhausted, and almost immediately, he must have fallen asleep. Even the fierce storm that was filling the boat with water (4:37) could not awaken him. The "frantic" (Mark's word) disciples finally wake him up shouting: *"Teacher, don't you even care that we are going to drown?"* (4:38). Then Jesus rebukes the wind and tells the water to *"Quiet down,"* using the same words he uses when he rebukes evil spirits and demands them to come out of a person. *And (the disciples) were filled with awe, and said among themselves, "Who is this man, that even the wind and the waves obey him?"* (4:41). He is the man who is always prepared for whatever winds and waves assault the day.

One of the things we know for certain was put in Jesus' agenda: *Then Jesus said, "Let's get away from the crowds a while and rest"* (Mark 6:31). As the Son of the Father, Jesus was able to calm a storm, as one who shared our humanity, he got tired, he found it necessary to rest. I have often heard the phrase, "He just goes like a house afire!" My response, if called for, is always: "I don't want to be around when he burns down." Recently, several articles have appeared discussing the problem of "burn out" among pastors. The warnings in these articles should not be limited to clergy; burn out appears to be almost epidemic. For many, life's demands have simply gotten too demanding. Jesus never accomplished less because he took time to be apart from the crowds and rest awhile; he accomplished more. Our effectiveness is lessened, our ability to persevere is reduced, and whatever satisfaction we find in our work is greatly diminished when we refuse to put into our daily schedules "the pauses that refresh".

Sometimes There Was a Plan to Follow

> *As they approached Jerusalem and came to Bethphage and Bethany at the Mount of Olives, Jesus sent two of his disciples, saying to them, "Go to the village ahead of you, and just as you enter it, you will find a colt tied there, which no one has ever ridden* (Mark 11:1-2).

Some things were a part of Jesus' planned agenda. Pre-arranged plans make this obvious. The Triumphal Entry donkey ride into Jerusalem was to be on a colt that had never been ridden and, Jesus, or one of his disciples had made the arrangement (Mark 11:1-2). Many who shouted "*Hosanna!*" that day were convinced Jesus, as Messiah, was about the make his move against Rome. ("Hosanna" literally means "save now".) Just as James and John had asked for seats of honor in the coming Kingdom, others appear to have forgotten what Jesus must have said on many occasions and repeated at his trial before Pilate, "*I am not an earthly king. My kingdom is not of this world*" (Luke 18:36).

Jesus was aware of, as were most of the those in the cheering crowd, the words in Zechariah 9:9 – *Rejoice greatly, O people of Zion! Shout in triumph, O people of Jerusalem! Look, your king is coming to you. He is righteous and victorious, yet he is humble, riding on a donkey – even on a donkey's colt.* Here was a different kind of Messiah and a different kind of Kingdom. (Note: This is why the more appropriate name for this day is "Passion Sunday," not "Palm Sunday.") Jesus had arranged a demonstration to align himself with Zechariah's prophecy. His movement was within Judaism, not extraneous to it.

> On reaching Jerusalem, Jesus entered the temple courts and began driving out those who were buying and selling there (Mark 11:15).

When you recall that Mark was written for Gentile readers, the cleansing of the Temple takes on additional meaning. Much planning was necessary for this assault on one of the Temple's chief moneymakers. For travelers (for which a fee was charged), animals for sacrifice had to be purchased. To pay the Temple tax, Roman money had to be changed to sanctuary coinage. "Doves could be bought cheaply enough outside, but the temple inspectors would advise worshippers to buy them at the temple stalls. Outside doves cost as little as 9 denarii, a pair, inside they cost as much as 15 shekels."[61]

---

61   William Barclay, *Mark* (Philadelphia: Westminster Press, 1956), 285.

Aside from the greed and *the den of thieves*, (better: *robbers*; Mark 11:17), the Temple had become, this market had been set up in the Court of the Gentiles, the only place a non-Jew could set foot in the Temple complex. In shutting out the Gentiles, Jesus holds this to be a violation of Scripture: *"My Temple will be a place of prayer for all nations"* (Mark 11:17). Following The Triumphal Entry, Mark records Jesus going to the Temple: *He looked around carefully at everything…* (11:11). One of the things he must have seen was "people carrying goods or implements, using the Temple as a short-cut when going between the city and the Mount of Olives. This had been forbidden by the Jewish authorities at the time, but the order was not being enforced."[62] If the Gentiles were to have a place in the Temple, this pathway and merchandizing market had to go.

Frequently, There is a Lesson to be Learned

"Leave her alone," Jesus said. "Why are you bothering her? She has done a beautiful thing to me" (Mark 14:6).

In telling the first story of Jesus the Messiah, Mark appears to be at full speed from beginning to end. He doesn't take much time setting the stage, but simply announces: *Here begins the Good News about Jesus the Messiah*, and brings John the Baptist on stage, preaching and baptizing. Although not apparent in many translations, one of his favorite words is *"immediately."* When John baptizes Jesus, the usual translation is: *when Jesus came up out of the water*. The literal Greek reads: *And going up from the water immediately, He saw the heavens being torn, and the Spirit coming down as a dove upon him* (1:10).[63] *"Immediately"* is also used in the following verses (KJV):

---

62 Kenneth S. Wuest, *Word Studies* (Grand Rapids: Wm. B. Eerdmans Publishing Co., 1961), 221.
63 Jay P. Green, Sr., ed., *The Interlinear Greek-English New Testament* (Peabody, Mass: Hendrickson Publishers, 1985).

- 1:12 – *immediately the Spirit drove him into the wilderness*
- 1:28 – *and immediately his frame spread abroad*
- 1:31 – *immediately the fever left her*
- 1:42 – *immediately the leprosy departed from him*
- 2:8 – *immediately when Jesus perceived in his spirit*
- 2:12 – *immediately he arose, took up his bed, and went forth*
- 4:5 – *immediately it sprang up*
- 4:15 – *Satan cometh immediately*
- 4:16 – *immediately receive it with gladness*
- 4:17 – *immediately they are offended*
- 4:29 – *immediately he putteth in the sickle*
- 5:2 – *immediately there met him out of the tombs*
- 5:30 – *immediately knowing in himself that virtue*
- 6:27 – *immediately the king sent an executioner*
- 6:50 – *immediately he talked with them*
- 10:52 – *immediately he received his sight*
- 14:43 – *and immediately, while he yet spake*
- 15:1 – *And immediately in the morning, the chief priests*

In the original ending of the Gospel (16:8), at the empty tomb, following the message from the angel, everyone is out of breath: *The women fled from the tomb, trembling and bewildered, saying nothing to anyone because they were too frightened to talk. The women rushed back to tell his eleven disciples – and everyone else – what had happened* (Luke 24:9). And, true to the spirit of Mark, *Peter ran to the tomb to look* (Luke 24:12).

Breaking into all this immediacy, and before the climax of Mark's story, there is a meal in Bethany at the home of Simon, a leper or a former leper. The story is in marked contrast to the tone of most of the Gospel. Perhaps this is Mark's method of calling our attention to a pivotal event that could easily be marginalized. During the supper, an anonymous woman comes in with *a beautiful jar of expensive perfume.* "It was a globular vase made of alabaster and containing an oil extracted from the nard plant native to India…

This imported luxury was costly: 'More than three hundred denarii' means approximately the annual wages of a rural day laborer."[64]

Some were indignant. "*Why was this expensive perfume wasted? She could have sold it for a small fortune and given the money to the poor!*" (14:4-5). Jesus rebukes the indignant and, according to the KJV, says: "*She has wrought a good work on me.*" What better captures the intent of his rebuke is best captured in what I believe to be a more accurate translation: "*She has done a beautiful thing to me*" (TNIV). One commentator writes: "Those who objected to the woman's extravagant act understood well the importance of giving to the poor, but they failed to see something even more important; the beauty and goodness of uncalculating love."[65]

The question raised by this episode might be phrased like this: Is there not a place in life for the beautiful and the extravagant offered in love? Jesus connected the anointing to his coming burial and noted that wherever the gospel is preached this act would be told in memory of this anonymous woman. This is how important Jesus considered what she had done.

Some Ramifications

The Basic Principle

> Psalm 37:5 NRSV – *Commit your way to the Lord; trust in him, and he will act.* Literally the word translated commit means roll so a good way to translate this verse is: *roll your life upon the Lord in utter abandon.* Do what you know you can do and ought to do and then let it go! "In the ancient Chinese Book of the Way...we find this piece of wisdom: 'Do your work, then step back.'"[66]

---

64 Lamar Williamson, Jr., *Mark* (Louisville: John Knox Press, 1983), 247-248.
65 Ibid, 249
66 Joan Chittister, *The Rule of Benedict* (New York: Crossroad, 1997), 36.

> Carolyn Myss said: "We are responsible not for the outcome of things, but only for the ingredients."[67]
>
> Coach Wooden writes in his autobiography that, despite his competitive nature, he always derived more satisfaction from coaching a team that lost while playing up to its full potential, than from a team that won while giving only a partial effort. To him the quality and intensity of effort was always more valuable than the results on the scoreboard. He defines success as the satisfaction of performing at maximum effort, to the limits of one's skill, regardless of the outcome. In his view, when maximum effort is given, there are no losers."[68]

It seems to me that the biblical requirement is not success, but faithfulness. That is the repeated word Jesus uses in his parables to describe those servants who receive commendations. With this priority for judgment, everyone can be a "winner." It is not necessary to cross the finish line first. It is enough to work with maximum effort to the limits of one's skill, regardless of the outcome. This allows us to focus on the ingredients and not on the outcome of things. It should encourage us to do our work and then step back.

You don't have to be at the head of the pack to be one of God's faithful servants. You don't have to worry about failure. You don't have to worry about feeling shame for the lack of some achievement. A brief conversation from a novel captures the real benefit:

> Jess said, "Life's messy, isn't it?"
> Newkirk had haunted eyes. "It's hard all right. But maybe a man can live with himself if he makes the right decisions. If he does what he knows is right. Things may not work out right, but at least he can live with himself."[69]

Even when things do not turn out exactly as we had hoped, there is satisfaction and peace in knowing that we gave it our best

---

67 Anne Lamott, *Plan B* (New York: Riverhead Books, 2005), 61.
68 Clifford Kuhn, *It All Starts With a Smile* (Louisville: Butler Books, 2007), 84-85.
69 C. J. Box, *Blue Heaven*, 345.

effort. At times, I wouldn't go so far as saying it had to be our maximum effort. Sometimes we're just not up to the maximum anything. That's a part of being fully human. Sometimes our best efforts mean the best we can do at the time under the circumstances. It's that "all things considered" aspect that certainly is a part of God's judgment on anything we do. He knows the limitations that life drops on us without a moment's notice. He knows when our less than perfect performance is the best we are going to be able to do at the time. Only God is able to judge how much effort goes into any endeavor.

The real tragedy in life is reflected in a Peanuts' episode that finds Lucy kneeling in her garden with Charlie Brown looking on. She says, "Boy, I'm gonna fool the birds this time." She stands up and stomps hard on the ground: "They won't get these flower seeds. I've really got those stupid birds licked this time." Then she leans over and whispers in Charlie Browns' ear: "I left the seeds in the package."

Some fear there is too much risk in planting the seeds of goodness, mercy, and compassion. Their lament is, "What's the use? The birds of prey are everywhere." The psalmist's words of wisdom speak to the contrary: *Don't worry about the wicked. Don't envy those who do wrong…Trust in the Lord and do good…Commit everything you do to the Lord. Trust him, and he will help you.* (Psalm 37:1, 3, 5). We are called to do what we can and let God take care of the rest.

Going With the Flow in the Here and Now

A river on a map is a simple thing. Our river starts at Trewsbury Mead, and follows a course of some two hundred and thirty-six miles to reach the sea at Shoeburyness. But anyone who takes the trouble to follow its route, whether by boat or on foot, cannot help being aware that, furlong by furlong, singleness of direction is not its most obvious feature. En route the river does not seem particularly intent on reaching its destination. Instead, it winds its way in time-wasting loops and diversions. Its changes of direction are frequently teasing: on its journey it heads at different times north, south, and west, as though it has forgotten its easterly destination – or put it aside for the while.[70]

Following this paragraph, I made a note that this is a good description of "going with the flow." It is certainly far from a gently floating downstream. I think it describes much of what Jesus encountered in his daily journeys with his disciples. The unexpected often appeared to rule the day. People showed up with all kinds of requests and demands. Mark's use of "immediately" paints anything but a leisurely stroll along quiet rural roads. Jesus certainly had various destinations in mind, but he was always prepared for the unexpected and the uninvited. Serendipity might be the best description of most of his journeys.

"Time-wasting loops and diversions" are often a part of the days of those of us who "go with the flow." We have certain places and even times in mind but who knows the people and the challenges that God may place in our path. We soon discover that many of life's interruptions are nothing less than opportunities we encounter in a daily journey to somewhere. In the process of caring for a flock of sheep, Moses stopped to see a bush that was engulfed in flames but not burning up. Exodus 3:4 tells us: *When the Lord saw that he had caught Moses' attention, God called to him from the bush, "Moses! Moses!"* I have often wondered how many times God has wanted to catch my attention in my hurrying through a day but I was not noticing life and happenings around me. I was too busy focused on where I was going that I failed to notice where I was.

When I read that Jesus asked his disciples, "*You have eyes -can't you see?"* (Mark 8:18), I shudder to think how many times he might have asked me the same question. Having an agenda with too much specificity can easily rob us of the specifics that God wants to include in our day. Too many of the people we just happen to run into, the book we just happen to pick up, the place or shop

---

70 Diane Setterfield, *Once Upon a River* (New York: Emily Bestler Books, 2018), 40-41.

we just happen to enter, the casual conversation we just happen to have with a perfect stranger – later do not seem to have "just happened," for they spoke to us in ways that made a difference in our day, and in some rare cases, in our lives.

Jesus' challenge to his disciples, both past and present, can frequently be summarized in two words: "*Stay awake!*" I don't like to consider how much time I have spent sleep-walking through life, not really being sensitive and alive to everything and everyone around me, my mind fixed on some other time or place. "Going with the flow" in my life has too often meant being focused on a destination or purpose to the expense of being fully-present and fully-alive where I happened to be at the moment. I remember a student who was part of a seminar I attended during graduate study in seminary. He always came in late, sat on the edge of his chair the entire time, and always left a little early. Unfortunately, I often saw myself in him: always coming from or going to, never present. It's difficult for God to get our attention when we're not really anywhere.

Timing is Everything

> Horace Greeley recounted a story that Lincoln told during his tumultuous passage through New York (on his way to his inauguration). Almost everyone he met was asking him if there was to be a war. Lincoln reached into his vast repertoire and told an anecdote about traveling through a country that had been flooded by rain, creating an endless succession of swollen rivers to cross. One of them, Fox River, was rumored to be larger and more dangerous than all the others and travelers panicked just thinking about it. Finally, about the Fox River. I have crossed it often and understand it well, but I have one rule with regard to Fox River: I never cross it till I reach it."[71]

You would be hard pressed to find a more exciting piece of historical writing than Ted Widmer's account of thirteen day rail-

---

71 Ted Widmer, *Lincoln on the Verge* (New York: Simon & Schuster Paperbacks, 2020), 349.

road trip to Washington, D.C. for Lincoln's inauguration. "Alan Pinkerton later claimed that the day before the journey was to begin, he received 'very decisive information' that Lincoln was to be assassinated in Baltimore.'"[72] Following Lincoln's election, states began to withdraw from the Union: South Carolina, December 20, 1860; Mississippi, January 9, 1861; Florida, January 10; Alabama, January 11; Georgia, January 19; Louisiana, January 26, and Texas, February 1.[73] "On February 9, two days before (Lincoln's) departure, a very different presidential election took place among the Confederate delegates meeting in Montgomery, Alabama. Jefferson Davis was easily elected."[74] It is easy to understand why everyone was asking Lincoln if there was going to be a war.

Lincoln was a master storyteller, especially for the right story at the right time. Lincoln's immediate task was to arrive safely in Washington, meeting as many people as possible along the way. That was his agenda and he did not intend to get lost in the future. I laughed at Lincoln's story and then was taken up short when I reflected on how many times I have crossed the Fox River before I reached it. Jesus gave his warning in Matthew 6:34: *"Don't worry about tomorrow, for tomorrow will bring its own worries. Today's trouble is enough for today."* Meeting each day as it comes with the best wisdom and resources we have is the best preparation for whatever comes tomorrow. If we are not careful we will find ourselves attempting to live several days at once which is just as impossible as trying to cross a river before we reach it.

A Verse to Remember

> Psalm 90:12 – *Teach us to make the most of our time, so that we may grow in wisdom.*

---

72 Ibid, 107.
73 Ibid, 31.
74 Ibid, 104.

CHAPTER NINE:

FULLY-HUMAN SPIRITUALITY ALWAYS INVOLVES "SPIRIT" WITH A CAPITAL "S"

THE BIBLICAL FOUNDATION

The Spirit is Foundational to Our Fully-Human Spirituality

> *Jesus replied, "The truth is, no one can enter the Kingdom of God without being born of water and the Spirit"* (John 3:5).

> *"Just as you can hear the wind but can't tell where it comes from or where it is going, so you can't explain how people are born of the Spirit"* (John 3:8).

> *"And I will ask the Father, and he will give you another Counselor, who will never leave you. He is the Holy Spirit, who leads into all truth. The world at large cannot receive him, because it isn't looking for him and doesn't recognize him. But you do, because he lives with you now and later will be in you"* (John 14:16-17).
> *"Oh, there is so much more I want to tell you, but you can't bear it now. When the Spirit of truth comes, he will guide you into all truth"* (John 16:13).

> *For all who are led by the Spirit of God are children of God* (Romans 8:14).
> *For his Spirit speaks to us deep in our hearts and tells us that we are God's children* (Romans 8:16).

> *And the Holy Spirit helps us in our distress. For we don't even know what we should pray for, nor how we should pray. But the Holy Spirit prays for us with groanings that cannot be expressed in words* (Romans 8:26).

When the Holy Spirit controls our lives he will produce this kind of fruit in us: love, joy, peace, patience, kindness, goodness, faithfulness, gentleness, and self-control (Galatians 5:22-23).

Do not stifle the Holy Spirit (1 Thessalonians 5:19).

A Misunderstanding from the Beginning

As much as we have heard it, you would think it would be everywhere in Scripture, but it is only found in John 3:5 and in I Peter 1:23. It is the phrase most often translated as "*born again*" that jolted Nicodemus and still jolts many of us today. On hearing Jesus' words as the call to be "*born again,*" Nicodemus asks, "*Can one enter a second time into his mother's womb and be born?*" Jesus immediately corrects him and says, "*You must be born from above.*" I believe things are a whole lot clearer when you translate the phrase "*born from above.*" It ties in much better with what Jesus says in John 3:8 – "*The wind blows where it chooses, and you hear the sound of it, but you do not know where it comes from or where it goes. So it is with everyone who is born of the Spirit.*" To be born from above is to be born of the Spirit.

The importance of Jesus' requirement to be born of the Spirit is underscored by something earlier mentioned that is most often lost to us. Our translation reads *the truth is*. In other translations you read verily, *verily, I say to you or truly, truly I say to you.* In the Greek text the word is *amen*. We usually think of this word at the end of something. It means to confirm, to give assent, to give a "so be it" to what another has said. Here Jesus puts it at the beginning of what he says. Literally he says, "*Amen, amen I say to you.*" There is no Jewish parallel for this. Twenty-five times we find this signpost in the Gospel of John; it is found only on the lips of Jesus. It is found three times in eleven verses in John 3.

Please note that Jesus says this to one of the best persons of his day: Nicodemus, a trained theologian. He was one of about 6,000 Pharisees who were dedicated to the keeping of the Law to the smallest detail. He was a good, devout man who came to Jesus at night. Some attack Nicodemus for sneaking in under the cover of darkness to talk with Jesus. But in that day, evening was the time set aside for busy men to study the Law after the day's work was done.[75]

Who is the Holy Spirit?

In the church calendar, the seventh Sunday after Easter is called Whitsunday or White Sunday because for centuries Christians dressed in white on that day to commemorate the coming of the Holy Spirit as recorded in Acts 2:4 – *And everyone present was filled with the Holy Spirit.* The complicated theory of the Trinity took four centuries to formulate: Father, Son, and Spirit…three "persons" of the "Godhead." My observation is that biblical theology is not so much reasoned out but lived out. The biblical writers are saying: "We experienced God as Father, Son, and Spirit."

And we remember that the Spirit of God is none other than God himself. The word for Spirit in both the Hebrew and Greek (both the Hebrew and Christian Scriptures) is the word for wind. The wind of God blows in his world as He is moving and active in it. Whether in the book of Exodus or in the book of Acts, the Spirit is simply the presence and power of God in the lives of people. The Holy Spirit is the Spirit of God.

What is really significant about Pentecost? I'm tempted to say that it is the only time in the history of the church that *they were all with one accord in one place* (Acts 2:1, KJV). Most modern translations render the verse as: *they were all together in one place* (TNIV). I believe this is truer to the text. The significance of Pentecost is *the roaring of a mighty windstorm in the skies above them, and it filled the house where they were meeting* (Acts 2:2). The wind/Spirit of God was present with them. This is why we write Spirit with a capital S. This is not the spirit of human beings (enthusiasm, etc.) but the Spirit of God, Holy Spirit as distinguished from any unholy spirit of the world. (In that day it was believed that the world was filled

---

75 Clifton J. Allen, ed., *The Broadman Bible Commentary,* Vol 9 (Nashville: Broadman Press, 1970), 240.

with many demon spirits.) The disciples did not perceive that the Spirit was some stranger or separate person called the Holy Spirit. They felt Jesus was back in their midst as he had promised.

I frequently answer the question, "Who is the Holy Spirit?" with three simple statements:

1. First, the Holy Spirit is the Spirit of God. The Bible plainly teaches a monotheistic faith; there is one God. From a practical standpoint some Christians are tritheists. The Holy Spirit is not a third party.
2. Second, the Holy Spirit is the Spirit of Jesus. If there is any key to begin to understanding the Holy Spirit, this is it. I say this because there has probably been too much emphasis on the phenomenon at Pentecost.
3. Third, the Holy Spirit is the Spirit of Truth. When someone asks me if I'm charismatic, I reply, "I hope so!" The word charismatic is used by Paul to mean "grace gifted." This basically means the style of life of a person who has received the grace of Christ. To have charisma, to be charismatic, is to be occupied by the Spirit of God, the Spirit of Christ, the Holy Spirit.

We Are Talking About Teaching and Guidance

"When the Father sends the Counselor as my representative – and by the Counselor I mean the Holy Spirit – he will teach you everything and remind you of everything I myself have told you" (John 14:26). Just as Jesus continued and clarified the work of God, so the Holy Spirit continues and clarifies the work of Jesus. Believers recognize the Spirit because his ministry is a continuation of the life and teaching of Jesus. To be occupied by the Spirit of Truth means truth as seen in the life and ministry of Jesus. To be filled with the Spirit is to be filled with his Way.

The word the KVJ translates "comforter" (John 14:16) is *paraclete*. Our translation above (NLT) translates it "*Counselor.*" Other, and I believe better translations than "comforter" are "Encourager and Advocate." The word *paraclete* means someone who is called in, one who is called in to help. Perhaps the best translation might be "Helper." That's who the Holy Spirit is: our Helper in seeking and finding truth. God helping us, Jesus helping us to live, to cope, to find our way, to find his way. The Holy Spirit is the Spirit of Truth about God, about ourselves, about life.

In John 16:13, Jesus tells his disciples that after three years of his teaching them as his disciples there is a great deal more he wishes he could have told them but it would have been too much for them to bear. Jesus adhered to the principle that ought to characterize all of our own "truth telling": Ephesians 4:15 – *Speaking the truth in love, we will in all things grow up into him who is the head, that is, Christ* (Ephesians 4:15; TNIV). It a sensitive and compassionate person to know when the truth will be edifying and transforming instead of crushing. I have rarely seen when "clobbering" people with the truth has been redemptive. Recognizing "teachable moments" is an art that brings about real growth.

Some Ramifications

The Basic Need

> He could see that she had once been a beautiful woman. She would be yet, he thought, except that something was missing. She was well-groomed. Her face was smooth and obviously cared for. Why wasn't she beautiful, or at least handsome? Because, he decided, she had no inner spark. Had she ever had it? He wondered. She was gracious and correct, but spiritless. It was as if that inner glow which gives vitality to the personality had been snuffed out. The spirit had been squeezed out of her.[76]

When I first read this paragraph, I immediately thought of I Thessalonians 5:19. The KJV reads: *Quench not the Spirit*. The NLT reads: *Do not stifle the Holy Spirit* which is in line with most modern

---

76 Charles Merrill Smith, *Reverend Randolph and the Splendid Samaritan* (New York: G. P. Putnam's Sons, 1986), 55-56.

translations. "Stifle" seems much the better word because "quench" implies "to extinguish," "to put out," meaning that the Holy Spirit is no longer a part of our lives. "Stifle" implies "to suppress," or "to ignore." The Spirit is still present but not in an active role in our lives; we have put the Spirit on the sidelines. We listen to our own voice rather to the Spirit's promptings.

Lucy, Linus, and Charlie Brown are playing in the sandpile:

> Lucy: I guess I have to leave…I hear my mother calling.
> Linus: I didn't hear anyone calling.
> C.B.: You should be glad you didn't. Her mother uses a whistle that only fuss-budgets can hear.

The Spirit uses a voice that only those who are receptive and open and listening can hear. You have to be tuned in. To live by the Spirit is to be listening to the Spirit, the Spirit of Christ, the Spirit of God, that inner voice. I don't believe God ever uses a megaphone or shouts to get our attention. I liken it more to the experience of Elijah in I Kings 19:9-13:

> "Go out and stand before me on the mountain," the Lord told him. And as Elijah stood there, the Lord passed by, and a mighty windstorm hit the mountain. It was such a terrible blast that the rocks were torn loose, but the Lord was not in the wind. After the wind there was an earthquake, but the Lord was not in the earthquake. And after the earthquake there was a fire, but the Lord was not in the fire. And after the fire there was the sound of a gentle whisper. When Elijah heard it, he wrapped his face in his cloak and went out and stood at the entrance to the cave.

It is so easy to stifle the Spirit's voice in our lives because often we are expecting God to be more dramatic and direct than "a gentle whisper." It's very difficult to keep the world turned down because it comes with mighty windstorms, earthquakes, and infernos. They certainly are attention grabbing and it takes no special gift to notice them. But finding a place, a time, and a mind-set to listen to the Spirit is a matter of deliberation and commitment.

Rather than talking a lot about spirituality, the Bible almost always speaks about being filled with the Spirit, being led by the Spirit, listening to the Spirit. I cannot find the source of this quote (I think it is Hans Kung), but I have never found a clearer presentation of what we mean by the Trinity: "Diagrammatically, it could be said: God the Father 'above' me, Jesus as the Son and brother 'beside' me, the Spirit of God and Jesus Christ 'in' me". This is why fully human biblical spirituality is always written with a capital S for Spirit. Even with all of our stifling, I don't believe the Spirit departs from us any more than God abandons us or Jesus refuses to walk beside us. Usually, as in the case of our illustration, the inner glow and vitality seem to seep out of our lives. It's almost as though the Spirit (capital S) has been squeezed out of us. But not really. I like to put it this way: our "stifling" simply pushes the Trinity to the outer recesses of our lives. They are always there, ready to reappear at our readiness and invitation.

Inner Strength Through the Holy Spirit

> *I pray that from his glorious, unlimited resources he will give you mighty inner strength through his Holy Spirit. And I pray that Christ will be more and more at home in your hearts as you trust in him. May your roots go down deep into the soil of God's marvelous love. And may you have the power to understand, as all God's people should, how wide, how long, how high, and how deep his love really is. May you experience the love of Christ, though it is so great you will never fully understand it. Then you will be filled with the fullness of life and power that comes from God.* (Ephesians 3:16-19).

In this verse we are talking about something that is not simply inspiration but something which is the energizer of our lives. We are talking about something within us which empowers us. We are talking about something within us which enlivens us. We are talking about the amazing power at work in us. This amazing power is the source of enthusiasm which ought to characterize the life of every believer. The word "enthusiasm" is from the Greek and literally means "filled with God." I submit to you that we need enthusiasm far more than we need inspiration. Enthusiasm has to do with our inner beings, the very heart and soul of life, the inner workings of who we are.

Henri Nouwen wrote a book for ministers but I am convinced his words apply to every believer:

> What needs to be guarded is the life of the Spirit within us. Especially we who want to witness to the presence of God's Spirit in the world need to tend the fire within with utmost care. It is not so strange than many ministers have become burnt-out cases, people who say many words and share many experiences, but in whom the fire of God's Spirit has died... Our first and foremost task is faithfully to care for the inward fire so that when it is really needed it can offer warmth and light to lost travelers.[77]

In a book with the subtitle "*Science, Faith, and How We Make Sense of Things,*" Alister McGrath provides a clear picture of the limitations of science and why faith has invaluable contributions to make to our lives:

> There are a number of statements that can be proved beyond doubt. Here are three of them:
>
> 2 + 2 = 4.
> The whole is greater than the part.
> The chemical formula for water is H2O.
>
> While these are all true, none of them can exactly be said to give us a reason for living. None gives us reason to wake up in the morning with a song in our heart or a sense of purpose in our lives.
>
> Christians believe that there is a God, whose loving presence and grace transform human nature and give us a reason to

---

[77] Henri J. M. Nouwen, *The Way of the Heart* (New York: The Seabury Press, 1981), 54-55

live and to hope. It cannot be proved. But it is a belief, which, if true, utterly transforms.[78]

The contributions made by faith are expressed this way:

> Roy Baumeister identified what themes had to be engaged and explored before the human quest for meaning could be satisfied:
>
> 1. The question of Identity: Who am I?
> 2. The question of Value: Do I matter?
> 3. The question of Purpose: Why am I here?
> 4. The question of Agency: Can I make a difference?
>
> (I would add a 5th: The question of the Future: Where am I going?)

> These are not empirical questions, which can be answered by the natural sciences…They lie beyond its intellectual horizons and methodological frontiers. Yet we cannot live with formulating answers to such questions.[79]

Most of us have come to believe that we are meant to live by inspiration. We are meant to fill our lives with slogans, quotes, and stories that provide motivation and courage for daily living. The problem with most of this is that it doesn't last very long and, more often than not, it is not very life-changing. The letter to the Ephesians was not written for super saints or for people who give their full time to religious matters. One of the reasons we can read a passage like Ephesians 3:16-19 and not feel a thrill of incredible possibilities is that somehow we feel it isn't really for the "average" believer (whoever and whatever that is). This letter was written to ALL of the believers in the church. It was written to "ordinary" people who had all the good qualities and all the weaknesses of church members in any time and any place. As a part of Holy Scripture, therefore, it was written for ALL of us.

---

78 Alister E. McGrath, *Surprised by Meaning* (Louisville: Westminster John Knox, 2011), 20.
79 Ibid, 105.

I now use Ephesians 3:20 as the benediction for the chapter and the reason why fully-human spirituality always "Spirit" with a capital "S":

> *Now glory be to God! By his mighty power at work in us, he is able to accomplish infinitely more than we would ever dare to ask or hope.*

A Verse to Remember

Psalm 100:2 – *Worship the Lord with gladness. Come before him, singing with joy.*

Chapter Ten:

Living in a Weedy World

The Biblical Foundation

Let Them Both Grow

> *Here is another story Jesus told: "The Kingdom of Heaven is like a farmer who planted good seed in his field. But that night as everyone slept, his enemy came and planted weeds among the wheat. When the crop began to grow and produce grain, the weeds also grew. The farmer's servants came and told him, "Sir, the field here you planted that good seed is full of weeds!"*
> *"An enemy has done it!" the farmer exclaimed.*
> *"Shall we pull out the weeds?" they asked.*
> *"He replied, 'No, you'll hurt the wheat if you do. Let both grow until the harvest. Then I will tell the harvesters to sort out the weeds and burn them and to put the what in the barn.'"* (Matthew 13:24-30).
> A Big Warning Preface: "Let's be clear, here. This story is not a call to be passive about the evils that we see. There are evils we clearly see in ourselves and in our systems that we can address and we'd better address."[80]

The parable cited above is a story about people who think they can get rid of the bad without doing any damage to the good. The meaning surfaces even with a first causal reading. The disciples ask Jesus in private: *"Explain to us the parable of the weeds in the field"* (13:36). There was one of two reasons for their question: Either they didn't get it OR they didn't like what they got. I suspect it is the latter of the two. It may not have been one of Jesus' more popular stories. It's only recorded in Matthew and most in the

---
80 Ronald J. Allen, *Theology for Preaching* (Nashville: Abingdon Press, 1997), 135.

popular culture have probably never heard it. The parable is about the way the world is and the way it is going to continue to be – and there is no way to fix things this side of eternity. Jesus' parable is a lesson in how things are: at the present time, in the Kingdom of God and in the world, there is a mixture of the good and the bad. In Jesus' explanation of the parable, he is the one who, at the time of harvest, *sends his angels, and they will remove from my Kingdom everything that causes sin and all who do evil…*(Matthew 13:41).

Many are seized by what one writer (Barbara Blaisdell) calls the "purity impulse":[81]

> Blaisdell warns that this is almost always a prideful impulse. Her challenge to this impulse speaks to the heart of the parable: "God is a strangely non-anxious farmer who tolerates conflicts and abides ambiguities until the growing is done. The parable raises a critical question. 'Can we trust such a God who will trust such a field?'"

Those who first heard the story understood the problem for dealing with the weeds too early in the growing season. The word for weed is "darnel" which is a weed that looks very much like wheat. In the early stages of growth, you can't tell the difference. If you go after weeds you might pull up the wheat by mistake. Another reason to curb the purity impulse, is that by the time the wheat and the darnel grow enough so that you are able to distinguish one from the other, the root systems are so entangled that if you attempt to pull up the weeds you will pull up a lot of wheat in the process.

Jesus' Explanation of the Parable

In the NRSV translation of the parable, the servants' lament is the cry that continues to be echoed in the world, "*Where did these weeds come from?*" (Matthew 13:27). The farmer's explanation is: "*An enemy has done it!*" When Jesus explains the parable to his disciples (13:36-43), he tells them that the enemy who sows weeds in the Kingdom field is the devil, Satan, the accuser, the adversary.

---

81   Ibid, 134.

He tells them that just as the Spirit of God is at work in the world for good, so there is another spirit at work in the world for evil. He doesn't explain why God permits this. He simply says it is the way things are.

William Barclay may be too basic for some but he remains a good source for a clear and basic understanding of a text. Here is what he views as the clear teaching of Matthew 13:36-43:[82]

1. It teaches that there is always a hostile power in the world, seeking and waiting to destroy the good see.
2. It teaches us how hard it is to distinguish between those who are in the Kingdom and those who are not.
3. It teaches us not to be so quick with our judgments. If the reapers had had their way, they would have tried to tear out the darnel, and the only result would have been that they would have they would have torn out the wheat as well.
4. It teaches that judgment does come in the end. Judgment is not hasty, but judgment does come. It teaches us that the only person with the right to judge is God. It is God alone who can discern the good and the bad.

Where the Emphasis in Scripture Lies

Don't let evil get the best of you, but conquer evil by doing good (Romans 12:21).

The sad commentary on the heresy hunts in the history of the church is that a lot of damage has been done to the field of the Kingdom. When the uprooting starts many are convinced it must be done. It is only at the end of the process that one can see how many good people have been uprooted in the process. And in the process of weeding there is often anger and arrogance and bitterness and resentment - all kinds of unloveliness which are totally out of character with what the Kingdom is all about.

It was Nietzsche who gave this warning: "Be careful, lest in fighting the dragon you become the dragon." How often has it been

---

[82] William Barclay, *Matthew,* vol 2 (Philadelphia: Westminster Press, 1958), 82-84.

that heresy hunters have become more destructive than the heresy they hunted. How often has it been that the weed pullers have just about destroyed the whole crop.

I don't want to push the story too far, but the purpose of the sowing is to get a crop of wheat. And if the people in the Kingdom of God are symbolized by the wheat, then the call for each of us is to be as "wheaty" as possible. To be real wheat; to look as much like wheat as possible; to really be those who can be spotted as citizens of the Kingdom of God, as disciples of Jesus Christ.

Stanley Hauerwas gives us a reminder: "A study of baptismal practice in the church's early history reminds us that anointing was a familiar practice. We also know that baptism was often referred to as illumination. At an early date in the church, we know that the newly baptized one was given a lighted candle and these words were spoken: 'You are the light of the world. Let your light shine.'"[83] I see our chief function to go into the world, not as weed pullers, but as light. The light that shines in the darkness – whatever and wherever that darkness may be.

SOME RAMIFICATIONS

An Illustration from History

> It was a hot day, with a high wind. Some men on the outskirts of the city had been burning Spanish moss, and the dry moss hanging from the trees caught fire and within seconds was out of control. When mother and her cousins climbed up on the roof to watch, nobody realized how totally out of control the flames were. The flames quickly spread from tree to tree and from house to house and it wasn't long until a terrified population was in the streets fleeing for their lives. It seemed so much like the end of the world that some were shouting, "Judgment day! Judgment day!" The good news was that they got rid of the Spanish moss but on that summer day in 1901

---

83 Stanley Hauerwas, *Sanctify Them in the Truth* (Nashville: Abingdon Press, 1998). 169.

they also destroyed just about the entire city of Jacksonville, Florida.[84]

The above anecdote is taken from The Crosswicks Journal – Book 2: *The Summer of the Great-grandmother*. It is the perfect picture of the consequences of ignoring the warning in Jesus' parable about not pulling the weeds: "In gathering the weeds you would uproot the wheat along with it." Preceding her relating the account, L'Engle calls it "the great fire of 1901 (that) destroyed the entire city of Jacksonville."[85] The fire quickly got out of control in the same way that weed-pulling can quickly get out of control with disastrous results. The history of the church is filled with the stories of well-meaning people (I'll give them the benefit of the doubt) who spotted weeds of heresy and felt called to be the eliminators. In the process, they usually eliminated and injured much other than the initially intended heresies. In these situations, collateral damage is inevitable and just how widespread it will be is unpredictable.

(A necessary sidebar: All three of the books in the series by Madeleine L'Engle are well-worth the read: *A Circle of Quiet; The Summer of the Great-Grandmother*, and *The Irrational Season*. I agree with Jean Kerr's comment on the back cover of Book 1: A Circle of Quiet: "My favorite of all Madeleine L'Engle's books. Lovely, charming, a book to cherish. I know it will give great consolation to ordinary people who sometimes wonder why they bother to get out of bed in the morning.")

A Matter of Reflection and Timing

> "My lady, we should just let them be for now," she whispered. "I know they're very wrong, but there are only two of us, and they've been drinking."
>
> Cecilia reluctantly nodded. Jane was quite right, of course. Two women against a group of drunken men might not end well at all. Cecilia knew she was often too impulsive, too quick

---

84 Madeleine L'Engle, *The Summer of the Great-Grandmother* (New York: HarperCollins, 1974), 212-214.
85 Ibid, 212.

to jump in, when cool, careful consideration, not to mention patience, would be more likely to win the day.[86]

It is all too easy to get caught up in the moment and yield to the temptation for immediate action. When a Samaritan village refuses hospitality for Jesus and his disciples, James and John ask Jesus: *"Lord, should we order down fire from heaven to burn them up?" But Jesus turned and rebuked them. So they went on to another village* (Luke 9:54-56). Evidently, they were not thinking very clearly about the kind of message this would send about Jesus, his mission, and his message. This incident would have spread like wildfire and cast the Kingdom about which Jesus preached too much in the light of the kingdom of Rome. They did not take time for careful consideration and certainly did not exercise any patience. Jesus' solution to this rejection was to go on to another village. Confrontation is not always appropriate and often unnecessary if the ultimate purpose is "to win the day." The end of Luke nine gives the request of James and John and In chapter ten Luke records Jesus' story of the "Good Samaritan." He goes on to another village in more ways than one.

Novels, especially British mysteries, often supply surprising insights into past cultures: "The village of Drim consisted of a huddle of houses with a general store at one end and the church at the other, a round church, because everyone knew that evil spirits could only live in corners."[87] Compare that assurance of where evil spirits could be found with this: "To the Jews, the Samaritans were a heretical and schismatic group of spurious worshipers of the God of Israel, who were detested even more than the pagans."[88] Contrary to our easily acceptance of the "good" Samaritan, very few Jews in Jesus' day believed that adjective could be applied to any Samaritan.

---

86 Eliza Casey, *Lady Rights a Wrong* (New York: Berkley Prime Crime, 2020), 40.

87 M. C. Beaton, *Death of a Ghost* (New York: Grand Central Publishing, 2018), 15.

88 John L. McKenzie, *Dictionary of the Bible* (New York: Macmillan Publishing Company, 1965), 765,

It is so easily assumed that weeds always look like weeds and evil spirits always look like evil spirits. The infamous Inquisition which began in 1232 to suppress heresy, soon became an instrument of torture in the hands of those who could spot a heretic a mile away. To be accused was almost tantamount to being convicted. That is one of the major dangers of all crusades.

The Basic Biblical Promise

When people are worried about what all those weeds, all those heresies, all that evil will do to God's wheat harvest, Walter Brueggemann, offers the best insight I have ever found based on this passage from Genesis 50:20 where Joseph speaks to his brothers: *"Even though you intended (hsb) to harm me, God intended (hsb) it for good, in order to preserve a numerous people has he is doing today."*

> "The plan of God" is a phrase that has been endlessly problematic in theological interpretation, as it has lent itself to all kinds of scholastic notions of a blueprint for determinism. Nonetheless, Israel does speak of Yahweh's *hsb*, which may be variously rendered "plan" or "thought," and which has the connotation of an enduring intentionality. As the narrative (about Joseph in Genesis) stands, it is only in retrospect that the narrator (or character in the narrative) can discern that Yahweh's powerful intentionality has been at work, not only through the vagaries of lived experience, but through the malicious intent of the brothers. In this usage, Yahweh's intention is a counter-intention that persists to override and defeat the deathly plan of the brothers. It is important that the affirmation is placed at the end of the narrative, for even Israel cannot know this certitude until it looks back on what has happened.[89]

My thesis is that God's enduring intentionality will not be thwarted by any number of weeds or any power of evil. The book of Revelation is the supreme statement that God's powerful intentionality will result in a new heaven and a new earth. Evil will not

---

89 Walter Brueggemann, *Theology of the Old Testament* (Minneapolis: Fortress Press, 1997), 355.

ultimately win out over good. Hate will not ultimately triumph over love. Falsehood will not ultimately destroy truth. Death will not ultimately have the last word; God will have the last word and his last word is life.

A Verse to Remember

> Psalm 31:21 – *Praise the Lord, for he has shown me his unfailing love. He kept me safe when my city was under attack.*

CONCLUSION:

Fully-Human Spirituality Involves the Uniqueness That Belongs to Each of Us

God has given us the ability to do certain things well (Romans 12:6).

Don't copy the behavior of and customs of the world, but let God transform you into a new person by changing the way you think. Then you will know what God wants you to do, and you will know how good and pleasing and perfect his will really is (Romans 12:2).

Now there are different kinds of spiritual gifts but it is the same Holy Spirit who is the source of all of them (1 Corinthians 12:5).

And in any event, you should desire the most helpful gifts. First, however, let me tell you something else that is better than any of them… There are three things that will endure – faith, hope, and love – and the greatest of these is love (1 Corinthians. 12:31; 13:13).

Does One Size Fit All?

Early in the ministry, there were two statements made about my calling that continue to give me pause. The first was made by someone when I was in my early twenties. Upon meeting her for the first time, the question soon surfaced: "And what do you do?" When I replied, "I am a minister," her comment was, "Well, you don't look like a minister." The logical comeback would have been the question, "What do you think a minister should look like?"

I didn't ask that question because it had never occurred to me that all ministers should look a particular way. We have all heard the remark about someone, "When God made _____ he threw away the mold." I can't find anywhere in Scripture that God ever had any molds when it comes to human beings. The above Scriptures indicate that callings and gifts are different and, further, seem to indicate that personalities are different. Fingerprints, eye prints, and voiceprints are unique for each individual which tells me that one size does not fit all. All ministers don't "look" the same. All _____ don't look the same (put in that blank any other calling, vocation, or whatever a person does for a living).

The second statement that remains in my minister's curiosity box was made many years ago. It followed one of the annual revival meetings in my boyhood home church after a particularly fiery, dramatic, Bible waving, and super-enthusiastic sermon presentation. An elderly member of the congregation proclaimed: "Now that's preaching." Well, it was one style of preaching and it was evidently what this man had learned to accept as the style.

So many factors (both conscious and subconscious) go into formulating what makes a "valid" profession, presentation, style, or technique. When a couple came to my office one day to complain that my preaching style was not like that of their former pastor (who had been the best at nearly everything), I confessed that was true. When they further explained what would be necessary for me to be the "right" kind of pastor, I realized it would have demanded a complete personality change. It just wasn't in me, it just wasn't me, to be and do what they were asking.

Whoever we are, wherever we are, and whenever we are (in time and culture), the challenge will always be to maintain authenticity and identity that is true to who we believe God has called us to be and how he is calling us to live out our lives. Uniqueness is built into each of us and the development of that uniqueness is what makes us who we are. Note: I'm not talking about some quirk or habit or desire simply to be different. I'm really talking about learning to be the best version of ourselves as God has created us.

I believe that when God transforms us into a new person (Romans 12:2), it is the person he always intended us to be. I can't look like all other ministers; I must look like myself. I cannot preach like all other pastors; I must preach in a way that is compatible with my grasp of the Gospel and my basic personality. I've lost the source, but I love this quote: "If I'm not going to be myself, who am I going to be?"

This certainly does not eliminate the need for growth and the continuing assessment of where and what we need to work on in our lives. We will always be works in progress, under construction, and subject to needed change. But this does not imply the goal of making ourselves fit a should and ought mold of conformity. A fully human spirituality is a spirituality that is truly us – flaws, blemishes, failings, weaknesses and loopholes included.

Uniquely and Always Imperfectly

Andrew Greeley was a Catholic priest, sociologist, and novelist who wrote what some consider unusual stories for one in his vocation. From his book, *Confessions of a Parish Priest*, come these insightful and instructive words:

> Fortunately, for me, my parents' emphasis on effort rather than outcome – and powerful praise for effort – dispensed me permanently from the obligation to be perfect. So I was freed by my parents, to a considerable extent anyway, of the need of perfectionism and of envious resentment of those who were better than I was…And more to the point, why should my work be evaluated against theirs? I write the kind of stories I can write and that I like to write, stories which I design to be comedies of grace…Why is it necessary to be Graham Greene or James Joyce? Why isn't it enough to be me?[90]

Greeley's confessions are almost a recital of the major themes we find in one who exhibits a fully human spirituality. He saved himself from the agony of comparisons by writing what he believed he could, should, and wanted to write. I cannot find anywhere in Scripture that an ingredient, in whatever shape and form final judgment takes, will be a comparison with others. With so many

---

90   Andrew Greeley, *Confessions of a Parish Priest* (New York: Simon and Schuster, 1986), 46-47.

variants, personal characteristics, and life experiences, how could any of us ever be compared with anyone else? I often like to say that comparisons are not only odious (courtesy of Evelyn Waugh), they are also frequently deadly. Some of the lines omitted in the above excerpt from Greeley echo my strong belief: "I am not James Joyce or Agatha Christie…In fact, one could fill the pages of a book with a list of authors and artists that I am not. But so what? Why need I be any of these people?"[91] To compare ourselves with persons who tower above us and assume we can grow to their stature is to dream an impossible dream.

Many years ago, I stumbled across a book with the arresting title: *Learning to Fall: The Blessings of an Imperfect Life*. The author is Philip Simmons who at age 35 was diagnosed with ALS, commonly known as Lou Gehrig's Disease. Among other things he writes:

> The challenge is to stand at the sink with your hands in the dishwater, fuming over a quarrel with your spouse, children at your back clamoring for attention, the radio blaring bad news, and say, "God is here, now, in this room, here in this dishwater, in this dirty spoon." Don't talk to me about flowers and sunshine and waterfalls: this is the ground, here, now, in all that is ordinary and imperfect, this is the ground in which life sows the seeds of our fulfillment.[92]

As I tried to think of a suitable benediction for this book, I could not get away from Simmons's challenge to abandon halo and hoverboard and live a fully human spirituality, a fully human life:[93]

> The imperfect is our paradise. Let us pray, then, that we do not shun the struggle. May we attend with mindfulness, generosity, and compassion to all that is broken in our lives. May we live fully in each flawed and too human moment, and thereby gain the victory.

Amen and amen.

---

91 Ibid, 47.
92 Philip Simmons, *Learning to Fall* (New York: Bantam Books, 2002), 37.
93 Ibid.

Bibliography of Quoted Sources

Albom, Mitch. *The Stranger in the Boat.* New York: Harper, 2021.

Allen, Clifton J., ed. *The Broadman Bible Commentary,* vol 9. Nashville: Broadman Press, 1970.

Allen, Ronald J., Blaisdell, Barbara Shires, and Johnston, Scott Black. *Theology for Preaching.* Nashville: Abingdon Press, 1997.

Aurelius, Marcus. *Meditations.* New York: The Modern Library, 2003.

Barclay, William. *The Gospel of John, vol 1.* Philadelphia: Westminster Press, 1956.

_____. *The Gospel of Mark.* Philadelphia: Westminster Press, 1956.

_____. *The Gospel of Matthew,* vol 2. Philadelphia: Westminster Press, 1958.

Barnstone, Willis. *The New Covenant.* New York: Riverhead Books, 2002.

Beaton, M. C. *Death of a Ghost.* New York: Grand Central Publishing, 2018.

_____. *Death of a Greedy Woman.* New York: Grand Central Publishing, 2011.

Box, C. J. *Blue Heaven.* New York: St. Martin's Press, 2007.

_____. *Breaking Point.* New York: G. P. Putnam's Sons, 2013.

Brueggemann, Walter. *Theology of the Old Testament.* Minneapolis: Fortress Press, 1997.

Buechner, Frederick. *Listening to Your Life.* New York: HarperSanFrancisco, 1992.

Callahan, Patti. *Once Upon a Wardrobe.* New York: Harper Muse, 2021.

Casey, Eliza. *Lady Rights a Wrong.* New York: Berkley Prime Club, 2020.

Cathcart, Thomas and Klein, Daniel. *Plato and a Platypus Walk into a Bar.* New York: Abrams Image, 2007.

Chittister, Joan. *The Rule of Benedict.* New York: Crossroad, 1997.

Ciholas, Paul. *Consider My Servant Job.* Peabody, Mass: Hendrickson Publishers, 1998.

Claypool, John. *Tracks of a Fellow Struggler.* Waco: Word Books, 1974.

Collier, Winn. *A Burning in My Bones.* Colorado Springs: Waterbrook, 2021.

Crane, Hamilton. *Starring Miss Seaton.* New York: Berkley Books, 1994.

Dalby, Robert. *A Piggly Wiggly Christmas.* New York: G. P. Putnam's Sons, 2010.

de Mello, Anthony. *The Song of the Bird.* New York: Image Books, 1984.

Douglas, J. D., ed. *The Illustrated Bible Dictionary, vol 1.* Wheaton: Tyndale House Publishers, 1980.

Gaebelein, Frank E., ed. *The Expositor's Bible Commentary,* vol 8. Grand Rapids: 1984.

Greeley, Andrew. *Confessions of a Parish Priest.* New York: Simon and Schuster, 1986.

Green, Sr., Jay P., ed. *The Interlinear Greek-English New Testament.* Peabody, Mass.: Hendrickson, 1985.

Hauerwas, Stanley. *Sanctify Them in the Truth.* Nashville: Abingdon Press, 1998.

Heller, David. *Just Build the Ark and the Animals Will Come.* New York: Villard Books, 1994.

Kuhn, Clifford. *It All Starts With a Smile.* Louisville: Butler Books, 2007.

Kushner, Harold. *When Bad Things Happen to a Good Person.* New York: Schocken Books, 2012.

Jung, C. G. *Answer to Job.* Princeton: Princeton University Press, 1958.

Lamott, Anne. *Plan B.* New York: Riverhead Books, 2005.

_____. *Stitches.* New York: Riverhead Books, 2013.

L'Engle, Madeleine. *The Summer of the Great-Grandmother.* New York: Harper   Collins, 1974.

Marlette, Doug. *The Bridge.* New York: HarperCollins, 2001.

McGrath, Alister E. *Surprised by Meaning.* Louisville: Westminster John Knox Press, 2011.

McKenzie, John. *Dictionary of the Bible.* New York: Macmillan Publishing Company, 1965.

Mills, Watson E. and Wilson, Richard F., eds. *The Mercer Commentary on the Old Testament.* Macon: Mercer University Press, 2003.

Nouwen, Henri. *The Way of the Heart.* New York: The Seabury Press 1981.

O'Day, Gail R. and Peterson, David L., eds. *Theological Bible Commentary.* Louisville: Westminster John Knox Press, 2009.

Palmer, Michael. *Resistant.* New York: St. Martin's Press, 2014.

Peck, Scott. *The Road Less Traveled.* New York: Touchstone, 1978.

Peterson, Eugene. *Leap Over a Wall.* New York: HarperSanFrancisco, 1997.

Schonfield, Hugh J. *The Original New Testament.* Shaftesbury, Dorset: Waterstone & Co., 1998.

Setterfield, Diane. *Once Upon a River.* New York: Emily Bestler Books, 2018.

Simmons, Philip. *Learning to Fall.* New York: Bantam Books, 2002.

Smith, Charles Merrill. *Reverend Randolph and the Splendid Samaritan.* New York: G. P. Putnam's Sons, 1986.

Sweet, Leonard. *Soulsunami.* Grand Rapids: Zondervan, 2001.

Taylor, Barbara Brown. *An Altar in the World.* New York: HarperOne, 2009.

Todd, Charles. *The Black Ascot.* New York: William Morrow, 2019.

Watson, Brian T. *Headed into the Abyss.* Swampscott, Mass: Anvilside Press, 2019.

Widmer, Ted. *Lincoln on the Verge.* New York: Simon & Schuster Paperbacks, 2020.

Williamson, Jr., Lamar. *Mark.* Louisville: John Knox Press, 1983.

Wilson, Andrew. *Shadow of the Titanic.* New York: Atria Paperback, 2011.

Wuest, Kenneth S. *Word Studies.* Grand Rapids: Wm. B. Eerdmans Publishing Co., 1961.

Yancey, Phillip. *What's So Amazing About Grace?* Grand Rapids: Zondervan, 1997.

www.ingramcontent.com/pod-product-compliance
Lightning Source LLC
LaVergne TN
LVHW041630070426
835507LV00008B/546